Wha

What's

so Fun-ny?

Humor is emotional chaos remembered in tranquility.
— JAMES THURBER

What's

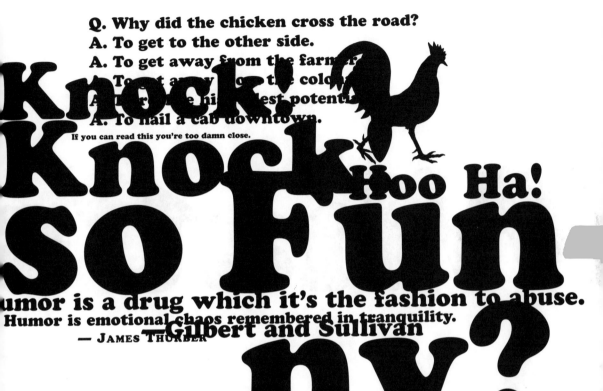

Q. Why did the chicken cross the road?
A. To get to the other side.
A. To get away from the farmer.
A. To get away from the colonel.
A. To reach his highest potential.
A. To hail a cab downtown.

If you can read this you're too damn close.

Knock!
Knock!
So Fun-
Hoo Ha!
umor is a drug which it's the fashion to abuse.
Humor is emotional chaos remembered in tranquility.
— JAMES THURBER —Gilbert and Sullivan
ny?

Har dee har har!
Does this typeface make my butt look fat?

47!

What's

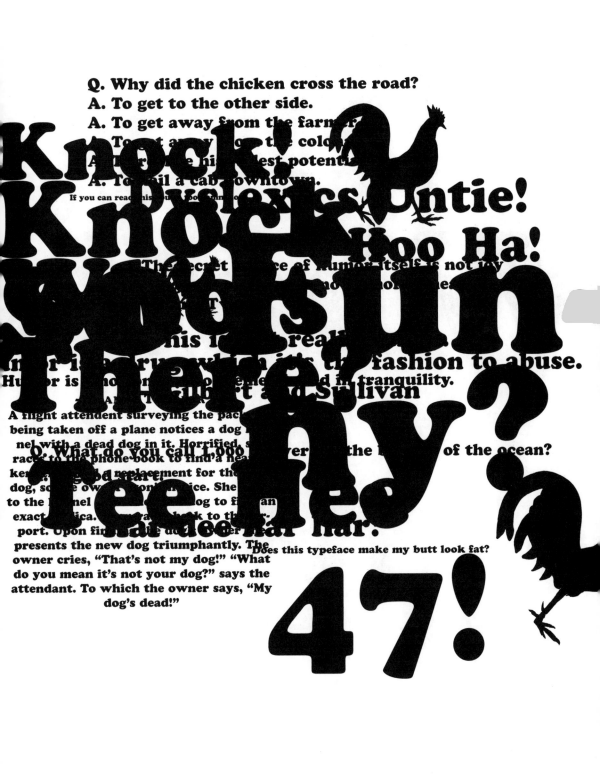

Q. Why did the chicken cross the road?
A. To get to the other side.
A. To get away from the farmer.
A. To get away from the colonel.
A. To reach his highest potential.
A. To hail a cab downtown.

If you can read this you're too close

Knock! Knock! Who's in There? Tee hee! Har har har! 47!

Dyslexics Untie!

Hoo Ha!

The secret source of humor itself is not joy but sorrow.

This is a break...

Humor is emotion remembered in tranquility.

Humor is... in its the fashion to abuse.

— Arthur Gilbert and Sullivan

A flight attendant surveying the pack being taken off a plane notices a dog nel with a dead dog in it. Horrified, s...
races to the phone-book to find a nea...
ken... a good replacement for the...
dog, so... the owner won't notice. She...
to the kennel to find a dog to fi... an exact replica... races back to the air...
port. Upon fin...ng the do... owner...
presents the new dog triumphantly. The
owner cries, "That's not my dog!" "What
do you mean it's not your dog?" says the
attendant. To which the owner says, "My
dog's dead!"

Q. What do you call 1,000... over... the... of the ocean?

Does this typeface make my butt look fat?

What's

Q. Why did the chicken cross the road?
A. To get to the other side.
A. To get away from the farmer.
A. To get away from the colonel.
A. To realize his fullest potential.
A. To hail a cab downtown.

Knock! Knock!

...

of the ocean?

when a politician is lying?

Does this typeface make my butt look fat?

47!

presents the new dog triumphantly. The owner cries, "That's not my dog!" "What do you mean it's not your dog?" says the attendant. To which the owner says, "My dog's dead!"

What's

Well, har de har har

Q. Why did the chicken cross the road?
A. To get to the other side.
A. To get away from the farmer.

Design Humor
The Art of Graphic Wit
By Steven Heller

ALLWORTH PRESS
NEW YORK

07 06 05 04 03 02   5 4 3 2 1

Published by Allworth Press
An imprint of Allworth Communications
10 East 23rd Street, New York, NY 10010

Researcher: Diana Litchfield
Cover design by James Victore
Interior design by Jennifer Moore, James Victore, James Victore, Inc.
Page composition/typography by SR Desktop Services, Ridge, NY

Library of Congress Cataloging-in-Publication Data
Heller, Steven.
    Design humor : the art of graphic wit / by Steven Heller.
          p.   cm.
    Includes index.
    ISBN 1-58115-246-9
    1. Wit and humor in art—History.   2. Wit and humor,
Pictorial—History.   3. Graphic arts—History.   I. Title.
NC1325.H45 2002
741.5'09—dc21

                                        2002010140

Printed in Canada

This book is dedicated to Harpo Marx, the silently frenetic clown, who relied on nuance and gesture to tickle the funny bone. To this he added a harp. Design humor relies on the same traits, more or less, minus the harp. If I were to design a typeface that embodied pure wit, I'd call it Harpo. But since I don't have the time or talent, my hat is off to the master of mime, maestro of mirth, and mentor of mimickry. Harpo is design humor incarnate.

his revised version would have been impossible if not for my researcher Diana Litchfield who kept a sense of humor throughout the entire process and brought insight and intelligence to the project. ❤ ❤ ❤ Thanks to Gail Anderson for being my co-author on *Graphic Wit*. And thanks to James Victore for his continued collaboration on this and other books. ❤ ❤ ❤ Of course, all the contributors who appear in the book are in my debt, or rather I'm in theirs, but who's to say. ❤ ❤ ❤ And warm gratitude to Tad Crawford, publisher; Nicole Potter, editor; and Jamie Kijowski, Liz Van Hoose, and Kate Lothman, associate editors at Allworth Press. ❤ ❤ ❤ ❤ ❤

I don't know what I'd do without you.

···SH.

2

32

xiii

xxiii

120

74

xv

96

xix

172

56

186

Table of Contents

Get a Grip!

Just in case some of you might say to the stranger sitting next to you, "Hey, I've read this book before and I want my money back damnit!" well, calm down, get a grip! There will be no refunds because you are only partially correct and therefore not entirely entitled to righteous indignation *or* financial remuneration.

This book is, in truth, a revised adaptation of *Graphic Wit: The Art of Humor in Design* by me and Gail Anderson (Watson Guptill, 1991), one of the best books that I ever produced, and one of my proudest accomplishments because humor is one of my favorite themes. Sadly for me (and YOU, I might add), the original version went out of print in 1996. Since another Johnny-come-lately book on design humor (which I refuse to name despite the pressure by my copy editor to squeeze it out of me) was issued by another publisher, I saw no pressing need to republish *Graphic Wit* until . . .

. . . until the phone rang about a year ago. You see, I've received a number of calls and e-mails from students (well at least three or maybe two, I can't remember) who are doing graduate thesis projects on graphic humor inquiring about the availability of the original book. Since these stalwart followers can't find it anywhere, I felt it was my duty (and my pleasure) to revise the original. But rather than merely add a few new paragraphs, a new picture or two, and emboss the cover with a gold-leaf label that announces "new and improved," this volume is considerably altered in various places and added to in others to reflect new tendencies, indeed a raging crisis, in graphic humor today. Well, maybe not a crisis as such, but there are new tendencies, at least I think there are. In any case, this book is unlike the original, except in some places, which if it really, really bothers you, I will exchange this book for an as yet undecided consolation prize, possibly my next opus, *Cool, Killer, Startling, Neat-o Everyday Hopefully Hip Graphics*. Though, trust me, you're better off with this. Seriously folks, this book is a respectful look at a difficult art.

I was inspired to write *Graphic Wit* after reading an earlier analysis titled *Visual Puns in Design: The Pun Used As a Communications Tool* by Eli Kince (Watson Guptill, 1982), the first book to my knowledge that defined and labeled the most common conceptual design practice. It concisely tracked how visual puns functioned, and how they were both similar to and different from the maligned verbal variety. Designers have employed puns since the invention of the modern trademark in Germany during the early twentieth century, if not before, but no one had given it a name. Paul Rand obliquely referred to puns in his informal discussions of "the play principle" but he was less concerned with nomenclature than with the manipulation of images and forms as a function of the overall play experience. He once told me that, "Without play, there would be no Picasso. Without play, there is no experimentation," adding that "I use the term play, but I mean coping with the problems of form and content, weighing relationships, establishing priorities." In any case, the pun is but a component of design humor, not the be-all or end-all of the design process.

When *Visual Puns in Design* first came out, I was a relentless verbal punster (I probably measured ten out of ten on the groan-meter for bad puns, though after therapy I'm better now). So I was very excited to learn from Mr. Kince that many visual concepts where rooted in the positive principles of punning. A pun-image offers a viewer-reader two or more simultaneous ideas that open to many additional levels of thought as it enhances the main concept. My favorite pun, for instance, is a logo for a restaurant called Mesa, which is spelled-out in gothic caps but the top of the letters are cut off in the form of, you guessed it, a mesa. This added dimension did not make the food any better but it did plant a mnemonic in my brain. The typeset word Mesa alone is not enough to spark recognition, but making the word into a pun gave it more resonance. The pun, I also learned is as endemic to conceptual graphic design as the metaphor is to creative writing. One aspect of design—and certainly logo design—is all about substituting a visual for a verbal concept, so I cannot imagine designers who are unable to marshal puns in their work—it is so common to design literacy. Yet puns are not the only humorous tool available to the designer. While this is not a revelation, it is a starting point from which to analyze other attributes of design humor. And this was the genesis of my own book and the beginning of a journey that would take me to the four corners of the world in search of the holy grails of graphic wit.

Once I started looking at graphic design with wit in mind, I found that humor derived from various stimuli. Some design was compositionally witty, or knee-slappingly funny as a result of shift in scale, odd juxtaposition, or simple repetition. Sometimes typefaces and typography evoked a simple smile or boisterous guffaw when expressively or metaphorically designed. Looking through Art Directors Club and AIGA annuals, I found that the most memorable work—regardless of subject, although subject plays a role—were those that evoked recognition through any or all of the characteristics mentioned. Humor, wit, and comedy, whatever one chooses to call it, has long been key to making graphic design more than the simple ordering of information or the beautifying of the commonplace. Humor is what makes design entertaining. And for all the high-minded sentiments—inherent in such notions as, "information architecture," and, "good design is good business," and, "design is a cultural force"—without the element of entertainment, a well-ordered and aesthetically pleasing piece of typography is ephemeral at best.

Humor makes design interesting for all parties, sender and receiver, designer and audience, client and designer, etcetera. As an art director, I enjoy solving problems addressing serious issues, but if I can inject humor into the solution I've made a real contribution. One of my favorite covers for *The New York Times Book Review* (see page 162) is one illustrating a few books about former President Clinton's embarrassing faux pas. As you will see, I asked an illustrator to parody the Beatles' "Sgt. Pepper's Lonely Hearts Club Band" album cover featuring all the accomplices in the scandals as a chorus behind Sgt. Clinton and company. He did a remarkable job too. Of course, parody is, in a way, the easiest kind of wit because it relies on an existing form, but when in clicks—when the concept sends up the original into a new realm of hilarity—recognition of the familiar is exactly what makes it ever more powerful and memorable. In the pantheon of design humor, however, the most original ideas are the icons. In fact, the original "Sgt. Pepper" album art was the true tour de force, a remarkable piece of design humor that may have built on the paradigm of a vaudeville stage or county fair show, but was totally transcendent.

It is not often that an author gets to revisit and remake a published book. But thanks to Allworth Press publisher, Tad Crawford, I have been given the chance to review a project that afforded me great satisfaction. I will not assert that this version is better, but it is very different. In fact, I've asked the designer, James Victore, to have as much fun with the design as his nervous system will allow. And, frankly, of this writing I'm uncertain what he's going to do. Whenever I call, he just snickers, "you'll see, you'll see." I know that with this much license to play one's tendency is to go berserk (as though the opportunity for unbridled humor will never happen again), but I presume Victore is able to deal with it. Whatever, from the raw material I have given him I expect that you and I will be paging through a comical experience, both restrained and excessive at times as suits his fancy.

However, if by the end you still feel like saying to anyone in earshot, "Hey, I've read this book before and I want my money back damnit!" I'll entertain your protestation as I laugh all the way to the bank.

—STEVEN HELLER

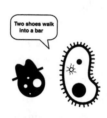

What's So Funny About Graphic Design

?

In the Beginning Was the Word

Actually, in the beginning there was paramecium. Then came pictures, and much later came words. But for purposes of developing the premise of this introduction, please allow me some latitude in condensing historical fact. This book is about words and images, and is replete with word-packed sentences about how words and images coexist as unified entities—as ideas. This book is about a very special aspect of graphic design, which I call *graphic wit* or *design humor*. While not all graphic design is witty or humorous, humor serves to enliven all visual experience, particularly graphic communications. Not all designers possess the ability to create truly witty or humorous work, yet the desire to be endowed with this gift is probably universal. Although I pride myself on having a good sense of humor, sadly, I have never mastered the art of humor in design. Therefore, I have concluded that graphic wit takes unique talents and distinct powers, and merits this book-length examination—indeed, personal analysis—of work created by my peers and betters over the past decade. Working within an historical context, Gail Anderson and I compiled a wide stylistic and conceptual range of such work, with the sincere hope that by presenting some of the most clever, ironic, and acerbic pieces from annuals, exhibitions, and designer's drawers, something other than ink might rub off on us—and on you, if you're so inclined.

Well-Chosen Words on Humor

Despite Mark Twain's assertion that "a classic is something that everybody wants to have read and nobody wants to read," his works, most of them written a century ago, are classics that virtually everyone *has* read and are indelibly etched into our minds. Twain's masterpieces are memorable not only for their appealing characters and compelling tales, but for the brilliant humor that underscores every aspect of his anecdotal prose. Twain's uncommon sense of the absurd gave him the power to make his readers appreciate both the lighter and darker sides of human foible and folly. Humor was his weapon and truth his shield, and implicit in his writing is the idea that we are all fools, with Twain himself at the head of the procession. Indeed, this self-effacing spinner of yarns employed all types of wit and humor—from jest to satire, slapstick to irony—making vivid pastiches by intuitively incorporating just the right quantities of reality and fantasy into his curiously honest representations of the society in which he lived (and sometimes suffered). Today, Twain is a paradigm of American humor, and his work is a basis for my assertion that humor is one of the two most powerful weapons a society can wield for good or evil (the other being fear).

By now you are wondering, if this is a book about *graphic* wit and design humor, why I should begin with a paean to a writer. Well, in addition to the fact that Mr. Twain is one of my favorite American authors, his example proves my claim that wit and humor—a distinction that will be discussed in due time—are the most important ingredients in any creative stew, particularly for creativity that strives for memorability, like graphic or advertising design. Twain, like many of this country's greatest verbal and visual humorists, proves that humor is the key to overriding our complex, internal security systems. Humor lowers defenses, releases steam, and excites the mind. Humor adds dimension to our experience and gives us great latitude in human affairs.

"Men will let you abuse them,"

wrote the nineteenth-century minister Henry Ward Beecher,

"if only you will make them laugh."

In fact, humor's cousin, laughter, has quantifiable curative benefits. Norman Cousins, who in 1982 wrote about overcoming disease through daily doses of humor, says that laughter triggers a secretion into the brain of a mood-enhancing chemistry that staves off depression. "Laughter is higher than all pain," wrote the late-nineteenth-century designer and social reformer Elbert Hubbard. Of course, laughter is also symptomatic of other, less joyful, emotions: "Excess of sorrow laughs. Excess of joy weeps," wrote William Blake, and the poet Byron said, " . . . if I laugh at any mortal thing, / 'Tis that I may not weep."

This should not surprise us—since humor and laughter are cousins, not twins, they will never have identical purposes or results.

But how do these distinctions relate to the subject at hand? Wit and humor in design—the playful manipulation of type and image separately or together—though sharing many fundamental attributes of verbal humor, are not encumbered by similar emotional complexities. Unhampered by the numerous light and dark psychological turns endemic to written or spoken humor, graphic design humor's primary agenda is to attract viewer attention and make a client's message memorable. How this is done is indeed varied and fascinating, but sometimes comparatively simple to achieve.

A Message from Dr. Freud

Before focusing exclusively on the historical manifestations and contemporary characteristics of wit and humor in design, it is important to explore briefly—and generally—the nature of wit and humor's effects on the funny bone (or their "relation to the subconscious," as Sigmund Freud said in his 1905 famous essay on jokes). Moreover, before we delve into realms exclusively visual and specifically graphic, we should define wit and humor, since the basic definitions are relevant to all media and forms. Rather than putting my faith entirely in Mr. Webster's dictionary definitions, however, I have consulted a few other experts for their opinions. With their help, I will first discuss humor, then wit.

James Thurber said, "Humor is emotional chaos remembered in tranquility," while Mark Twain wrote, "The secret source of humor is not joy, but sorrow." Cartoonist and author Don Herold tells us, "The nearer humor is to pain, the longer it is apt to last." And journalist Kenneth Bird coined the old chestnut that goes, "Humor is falling downstairs if you do it while in the act of warning your wife not to." Turning to the dictionary, we are told that "humor is a changing (or fluid) state of mind"—which is exactly what one would expect from a cool dictionary definition. So I prefer Groucho Marx, who, though no more precise than Mr. Webster, is much warmer when he says, "There are all kinds of humor. Some is derisive, some sympathetic, and some merely whimsical."

According to these experts, humor is a combination of actions and reactions, often rooted in turmoil. Nevertheless, they all seem to find it either too complicated to define precisely (or perhaps they feel it is unnecessary to do so). In *Enjoyment of Laughter*, a definitive 1936 text on the subject of jokes, Max Eastman says rather nondefinitively, "Humor at its best is a somewhat fluid and transitory element." But even if we could all agree on a universal definition, would this intellectualizing enhance our appreciation of humor? Isn't it true that if we analyze—or vivisect —a joke, verbal or visual, it then loses its specialness and is therefore no longer funny? Humor, after all, relies on the unexpected—a clinical explanation of humor would reduce the element of surprise. Eastman asserts that "a study of the classification of the kinds of humorous experience on the basis of theory as to its nature is a . . . science . . . [but] it is not, to be sure, a vitally important science." Understanding the distinction between good and bad humor, he argues, does not ensure that one's sense of humor or one's ability to tell a joke will improve. Therefore, as unscientific as it may sound, I've concluded that humor is in the genes at birth, and is sparked by the instinct for play that all children have.

Classic humor will always be funny despite the folly of those pedants (like myself) who try to analyze it. For this humor is neither topical nor fashionable but timeless and true. I cannot remember how often I have seen and laughed at the same jokes over and over in my favorite films, such as the Marx Brothers' *Duck Soup* and Woody Allen's *Annie Hall*. Or, for that matter, at the vintage advertisements, like George Lois's 1962 Wolfschmidt's Vodka campaign and Helmut Krone's 1960 Volkswagen "Lemon" campaign, which are so conceptually astute—and have become so paradigmatic of their genre—that I continue to be awed by their brilliant yet simple humor. Since I hate the old adage, "I don't know what humor is, but I know it when it hits me," I shall give you this explanation of humor by author Howard Brubaker and offer it as my own: "[T]he common denominator of humor is the contact of incongruous ideas. This mixture causes a series of little explosions as in an internal combustion engine."

If humor is like fuel, then wit, said George Herbert, "is at times an unruly engine." As the word phonetically suggests, wit is fast paced—a swift perception, usually of the incongruous. In contrast to a less sophisticated form of humor, like jest, which Sigmund Freud describes as "nonsensical comic relationships made by children or childlike adults for the purpose of pure pleasure," wit is the ability to control incongruous or nonsensical stimuli for purposes of tapping into deeper reservoirs of human experience.

Unlike play, a rather joyful and random activity that is key to all humor, wit involves a greater degree of cleverness and sarcasm. Wit, therefore, runs the risk of being too self-conscious—being witty can be both a gift and curse. For the nineteenth-century critic William Hazlitt, "Wit is the salt of conversation, not the food." Though I fundamentally disagree with the notion that wit is merely seasoning for a greater intellectual feast, I do seriously consider the validity of the following statement, made a few centuries earlier by the philosopher John Lyly in *Anatomy of Wit*: "I have ever thought so superstitiously of wit, that I fear I have committed idolatry against wisdom." I believe that while some wit has a foothold in wisdom, wit can also be misused and misdirected. Not too long ago, novelist Geoffrey Bocca brilliantly described wit as "a treacherous dart. It is perhaps the only weapon with which it is possible to stab oneself in the back."

Effortless Complexity

True wit, though volatile, depends on the mastery of various forms of language. The witty writer, for example, is a verbal acrobat whose high-wire antics rely on precise timing and acute understanding. No matter how precarious the death-defying feat, this writer must land perfectly on his or her feet. The great humorous writers are known for crafting figures of speech into vivid mental pictures. As a classic example, let's take the phrase *dog bites man*, which is neither funny nor news. Conversely, *man bites dog* is both news and somewhat funny because it twists the ordinary. But, more to the point, *man bites man* is not only a surprising concept but at once a vividly absurd picture revealing two simultaneous concepts. At the risk of committing *humorcide* through overanalysis, I submit that in this phrase one man is not only physically assaulting the other in a rather annoying and unconventional manner, but that since the word bite also suggests ridicule or criticism, it gives the phrase an additional level of meaning, causing it to be even funnier than its literal content suggests. Another example of such skillful verbal wit comes from Max Eastman, who quoted a young World War I soldier after the latter's first visit to Paris's legendary *Folies Bergere*:

"I never saw such sad faces or such gay behinds."

In addition to having the sting of a sound-bite, this is a sage observation conjuring a real-life portrait of the vivacious but overworked sex objects who danced the famous Can Can night after endless night in the Parisian nightclub. What these examples suggest is that the most skillful wit must appear effortless while being loaded with meaning. Even Aesop said something to the effect that "clumsy humor is no joke."

Low Humor/High Wit

Graphic wit should be no exception. The best design solutions must appear not only effortless but free from the self-conscious and tired conceits of all belabored humor. Yet if this is true, then why is it that the pun is one of the most significant components of graphic wit and design humor? As the oldest form of humor, the pun is also considered in the world of letters—as in the world—to be the lowest form. There is no kind of false wit that has been ridiculed as much as the pun, said one critic. Yet a pun, the dictionary tells us, is "the humorous use of a word or words which are formed or sound alike but have different meanings, in such a way as to play on two or more of the possible applications; a pun is a play on words." Though the theory is sound, Edgar Allan

Poe complained about the practice that "the goodness of the true pun is in the direct ratio of its intolerability." An old English proverb goes, "Who makes a pun will pick a pocket." And who can forget that old grade-school put-down, "*PU* is two-thirds of a pun." Indeed, throughout the ages this venerable form has been so abused that the *New York Times* forbids puns in its headlines unless the word substitution is so inextricably linked to the meaning of the story that the pun is incidental.

However, to answer the question of why puns are necessary in graphic wit and humor, one must understand that the rules that govern verbal language do not translate precisely into visual language. Thus, the *New York Times* has no rules governing visual puns. Graphic designers' canon of usage is different because our means of communication—our language, syntax, and grammar—are different. A picture is worth a thousand words because so much more information can be evoked through one image than in a sentence or paragraph. In visual language, it often is necessary to substitute one image for another, or one symbol for another—not just for purposes of jest, but to enhance meaning. Therefore, the pun—at best a kind of shorthand, at worst a strained contortion—describes graphic symbols used to simplify complex concepts into accessible, often memorable images.

Paul Rand, in *A Designer's Art* (Yale University Press, 1985), says visual puns are the keys to some of his most successful designs, since "they amuse as they inform." The elevation of the pun from jest to graphic communications tool must also be credited to one of Rand's former Yale University students, Eli Kince, whose *Visual Puns in Design* (Watson-Guptill, 1982) argues that a pun is the conveyor of credible visual messages. If the pun is the lowest form of verbal humor, Kince reasons, this may beg the question, "Is graphic humor at the low end of the evolutionary scale?" Kince quotes Charles Lamb saying puns are "a pistol let off at the ear, not a feather to tickle the intellect." Remember too that the best verbal puns are not simple-minded rhymes but truly surprising (even shocking), yet decidedly logical, manipulations of language. So at the risk of sounding hyperbolic, the best visual puns have a similar effect on perception as, say, a right cross to the chin, for the result is indeed staggering. With the logo for *Families* magazine, the late typemaster Herb Lubalin created a rather literal symbol for *family* out of the letters *ili*, resulting in a memorable icon. For the reader or viewer, it was also a rebus,

which, when recognized, added another level of appreciation. When a visual pun works—specifically, when two distinct entities merge to form one idea—the effect stimulates thought and sensation.

Measuring What's Funny

The first law of humor that Max Eastman quotes in *Enjoyment of Laughter* is that "things can be funny only when we are in fun." There may be a serious thought or motive lurking underneath our humor. We may be only "half in fun" and still be funny. But when we do not have the spirit of fun at all, when we are, as Eastman warns, "in dead earnest," humor is the thing that is dead. This implies a distinction between fun and funny, an idea dating back to ancient Greek theater (in fact, much of what we call comic can be traced to this source), when irony was first used as a means to teach moral tales. Though the messages were serious, indeed tragic, the means to achieve catharsis were often conveyed through humor – a humor that shed light on the truth.

Groucho Marx's description of diversity in verbal humor, applies as well to graphic wit and humor, but one difference between verbal and design humor is apparent: the latter cannot always be measured by laughter alone. In fact, I doubt that anyone reading or looking at the images in this book would double over from laughter, because that is not the nature of graphic design humor. As a selling tool, graphic design humor might be described as a loss leader—a means to grab attention and lure the customer or client into the store. Humor, then, cannot be too outrageous, lest the purpose be defeated. Even as a political weapon, humor similarly functions to sell a message, sometimes by ridicule, but is often subtle or sardonic, not ripsnortingly funny. At best, humorous design will force a laugh, bring a smile, or cause a double take, which is nothing to be ashamed of. Indeed, like hypnotic suggestions, the goal of graphic wit and design humor is to *subvert* the subconscious and thereby earn a market share of memory. If, for example, Milton Glaser had designed his "I ♥ New York" trademark using an elegant typeface and spelling the word *love*, it would be humorless, and probably unmemorable; instead he created "I ♥ New York," which, although not a sidesplitter, is a witty combination of word and symbol that today is a much-imitated visual device. After the terror attack of 9/11, the symbol had an even greater, indeed serious, significance when Glaser included the words, "More than ever" on the I ♥ NY logo and further added a dark stain to the lower left-hand portion of the heart to represent the destruction of the World Trade Center and over three thousand victims. The revised symbol retained its wit while its message transcended the lighthearted intent of the original.

Humor is a mnemonic tool—something that helps (or forces) us to recollect. This can be manifest in *wordplay*, like a slogan or jingle, or *picture play*, such as a logo or trademark. An example of the former is the brilliant slogan for *New York Newsday*: "On Top of the News and Ahead of the Times." In that simple phrase, *Newsday* memorably positions itself as both a superlative newspaper and worthy competitor. On first reading *On Top of the News* implies breaking its share of news stories, while *Ahead of the Times* implies being progressive but not doggedly fashionable. But it also invokes the claim the *Newsday* is better than the *New York Times* and the *New York Daily News*. An historical example of picture play is a three-panel Dubonnet poster designed by A. M. Cassandre in 1932, which even today is memorable for its playful wit. In his marriage of word and image, Cassandre's comic trade character, the

"Dubonnet Man," sits drinking the wine at a café table. In panel one, he is rendered mostly in outline, his partially painted arm outstretched with glass in hand; underneath, the work DUBONNET is rendered half in bold, the rest in outline, focusing the viewer's eye on DUBO. In the second panel, the character is drinking as his outlined body begins to fill with color and detail, and another letter, the N, is now bold, revealing DUBON. And in the last panel a completely rendered character is pouring from a bottle to refill his glass, and the DUBONNET is completely bold. This brilliant visual "jingle" has multiple levels of meaning: in French, *dubo* means "something liquid," *dubon* means "something good," and Dubonnet is indeed a wonderful wine. The fast cadence of *DUBO, DUBON, DUBONNET* is appealing for its almost rhythmic syncopation, but there is something else going on here—in addition to the sophisticated verbal and graphic tricks, Cassandre used a more fundamental aspect of humor to achieve the final result, an activity called the play principle.

In *Thoughts of Design*, Paul Rand asserts that play is essential to the practice of all graphic design. Play is a kind of abandon, yet, as we know from small children, play is their work. In the initial stages of a project (and possibly throughout), the designer ostensibly becomes an adult child, allowing attachments to shift capriciously from one plaything to another. In design, however, playthings are type and image, which are really puzzle pieces to be more or less instinctively moved, juxtaposed, and even mangled and distorted until a serendipitous relationship between formal and contextual problems is achieved. Even the most rigidly systematic design solutions are born of play.

"Humor, is play,"

said Max Eastman. Though all humor derives from play, play does not always result in humor. The play principle in design involves intuition, and intuition is a switch that starts and stops the play process, controlling when a designer will move from childlike abandon into adultlike premeditation. What we will call design intuition is not, however, a parapsychological force, heavenly gift, or atavistic trait, but rather a mixture of unreasoned and learned knowledge. Indeed, one way to describe design is as equal parts play and intuition, dictated by the requisites of the problem at hand,

and play alone cannot be considered design in the formal sense until an overriding intelligence puts the variables into some kind of order. Moreover, though born of play, graphic design is not inherently humorous. Design humor is the deliberate merging of incongruities into some kind of credible communication that is not overshadowed by reason but is nevertheless governed by it. Wit and humor in design occur when play and logic are seamlessly intertwined.

Not Every Designer a Humorist

I am not a humorous designer, at least given the standard that the best visual humor is surprising, fresh, and unencumbered by cliché. Indeed, many otherwise very talented graphic designers are unable to translate good verbal sense of humor into visual humor—some have the knack, others do not. This book is replete with examples of those who do. But even in this compilation, the qualitative range varies. The exemplars are those who invent new forms rather than conforming to tried and true formulae. They might take chances with subjects and themes that have traditionally defied humorous treatment, like annual reports, and they realize that the easy solution is not necessarily the best, and that effective humor is not always an easy solution.

While I will attempt to "deconstruct" the process of wit and humor in design in this book, there are no correct formulae. Do not read it with the idea that this is *Graphic Comedy 101*. For though humor can be explained, it cannot be taught. While certain formal characteristics are common to all humor in design, like exaggerated scale, odd juxtapositions, and ironic relationships, these same traits also apply to "straight" design. To be certain, a big head placed atop a little body does not ensure hilarity, and a piece of nostalgic clip art used in a work does not *a priori* make it funny. Humor in design is an art, not a procedure. With that in mind, this book will not make a serious designer funny, nor a funny designer an even brighter wit; it will, however, examine a range of ideas and forms in the work of others, so that even if we cannot be great graphic humorists, we can appreciate those who are.

HUMOR IS ONE OF THOSE FAST-ACTING TRANSPARENT **DELIVERY SYSTEMS THAT** EASES THE CONCEPT TO THE BRAIN. **IT'S ABSORBED** SEEMINGLY EFFORTLESSLY AND GIVES GREAT PLEASURE, **AT THE SAME TIME.**

Steven Guarnaccia

HUMOR IS RELIEF FROM THE ANXIETY THAT THE HUMAN CONDITION GENERATES.

Seymour Chwast

makes you feel good all over and glad to be alive.

Bonnie Siegler and Emily Oberman

Chapter

1

Anatomy of Wit

Dissecting humor can be a perilous activity. Wit and humor are fragile at best, with overanalysis often resulting in witless and humorless conclusions. Therefore, the purpose of this section is not to disassemble witty or humorous design into its component parts, but to explore some fundamental formal and stylistic characteristics common to all types of graphic design, especially those witty and humorous.

Prehistoric Humor

The origins of visual humor might be traceable to the platypus, whose prehistoric ancestor emerged from the slime millions of years ago near what is now northern Australia. This aquatic mammal with beaver body and duckbill face was possibly Mother Nature's attempt at a visual joke. If this seems a cruel assessment, then consider the suggestion that she was playing with random forms, not unlike a designer sketching an initial idea, never intending to end with this design until seriously smitten by the platypus's comic physiognomy. However, it's no joke that prehistoric man applied his humor primarily to animals—the first true graphic wit was probably represented in depictions of animals on the walls of early cave dwellings. Evidence at Lascaux and other caves indicate man's first attempt at interpretative and caricatural art in the form of drawings of local animals.

Holy Humor

A brief examination of the roots of contemporary graphic wit and design humor reveals that the basic methods for achieving visual humor have not been radically

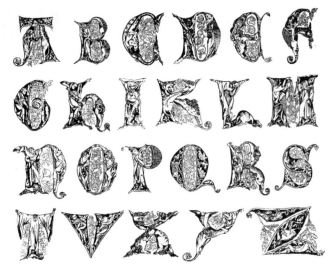

Medieval illuminated alphabet (date unknown).

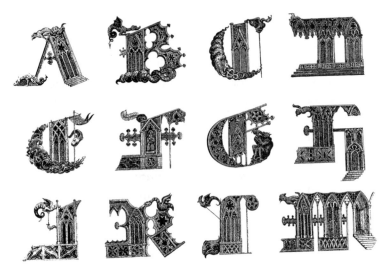

Illuminated alphabet made from medieval architecture (c.1830s).

altered in ages. Early graphic wit can be traced back to anthropomorphized animals that were given symbolic guises by renegade social critics, who used them to represent aspects of human folly. However, the earliest of what we shall loosely refer to as graphic design humor originated in early Christian illuminated manuscripts, prayer books, and psalters from around the eighth century. These are the first examples of the primary graphic design ingredient, the letterform, being seamlessly tied to an image. (For an excellent discussion on this subject, read *Letter and Image* by Massin [Van Nostrand Reinhold, 1970].) It is in these odes to the Word that scribes made

Medieval illuminated alphabet (date unknown).

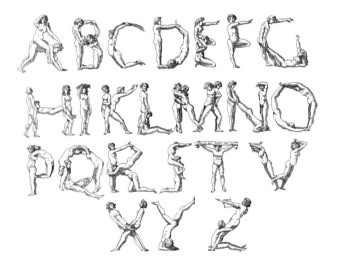

Nineteenth-century anatomical alphabet (1834).

letters out of drawings of contorted human bodies and animal forms that were sometimes realistic, sometimes fantastic, but often quite funny. Some illuminations were serious symbolic interpretations of holy scripture, while others were just grotesque or ridiculous juxtapositions conceived for the scribe's simple pleasure of constructing a fanciful letter.

Dragons and serpents slithered their way into manuscripts during the ninth century, their scales, tails, and tendrils interweaving with the text in sometimes illegible compositions. Likewise, pictures of exotic vegetation and foliage, witty in terms of

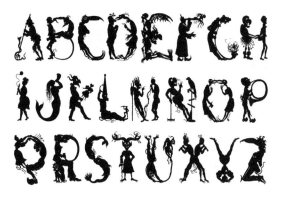

Figurative alphabets of comic vignettes (c.1830).

their placement on the page, began growing like kudzu on other manuscripts of the same period. Eventually, these intricate visual decorations evolved from truly biblical allegories and symbols into nightmarish creatures, including quadrupeds with human heads, two-headed birds or griffins, humans with paws, plants with beaks, and winged cattle—similar to medieval gargoyles, which anticipated nineteenth-century surrealistic imagery. Many of these initials and marginal decorations had no relationship whatsoever to their texts, and it seems that the illuminators (or designers) were not just being comic or playful, but delinquent in their duties. Actually, Massin writes that the scribes and illuminators from different monasteries competed with each other, as if in some obsessively perverse design competition, to see who might achieve the most outrageous visual folly.

Nineteenth-century anthropomorphic letters (c.1840).

In the fourteenth century, a backlash against this trend toward visual farce was initiated by the leading clerics, who established a canon for the proper illumination of sanctified manuscripts. And for a short period, graphic humor was controlled, if not eliminated entirely. With the perfection of woodblock and copperplate engraving around the fifteenth century, letterforms once again became comic in theme though rigid in form, in part owing to strictures imposed by the media. Contrasted to earlier outrageous designs, which extended beyond the letterform confines into the page margins and text areas, these subsequent engraved illuminations told an entire visual story within self-contained letterforms known as *casket letters*. These initials prefigured the fancy faces and novelty typography of the late nineteenth century.

Earthly Humor

In the fourteenth century, Romanesque and Gothic architectural styles were mimicked in period letterforms. The former organically wed excessive ornament to function; the latter featured minimal ornament with a purely formal or aesthetic role. With both, however, visual humor of the kind found in architectural decoration was frequently replicated in the letters. During the middle to late Renaissance, the rules of geometry began influencing concepts of beauty, and so governed the infant art of typography, which as one of its tenets rejected overly decorated (and, by extension, humorous) letterforms. Eventually, the Romanesque, Gothic, and later even Baroque modes of decorative lettering became popular in books and other forms of printing, ultimately influencing a style of humorous graphics found centuries later in commercial typography and design.

During the long interval between the sixteenth and nineteenth centuries, technological and commercial advances significantly altered the role of graphics in society from elitist to populist. Hence, graphic humor became more varied. The communications history of the nineteenth century was heavily molded by the confluence of political, social, and technological advancements. This period of both flowering enlightenment and strict repression had a strong impact on visual humor.

In the 1830s, the development of commercial printing methods, particularly lithography, afforded graphic artists new freedoms of expression and fresh outlets for their talents. Lithography offered greater production flexibility, resulting in low-cost printing for increased quantities. And new distribution methods allowed for greater circulation of what was produced. The most fascinating graphic humor at this time, however, was not found in mass periodicals, as one might expect, but rather in a curious medium: children's alphabet primers. Progressive educators determined that rather than forcing the study of language on youngsters who were more inclined to play than learn, the inclusion of comic visual "games" in their lessons, including metamorphosed alphabets and rebuses, would provide essential learning aids while children played. Similar typographic playfulness was, of course, prevalent in adult-oriented literature in the form of surrealistic and comic initial letters.

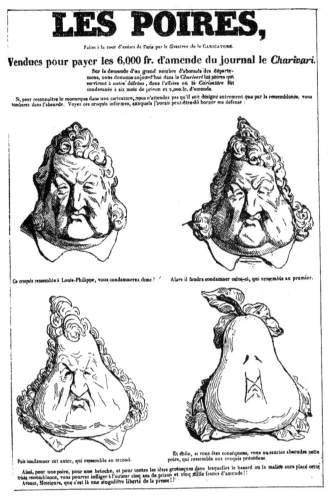

Les Poires (Pears) wherein Charles Philipon transforms French monarch
Louis-Philippe into the Pear King (1834).

The most important outlets for expressive, comic, and satiric graphic art during
this time were newspapers in France, the most noteworthy of which was the weekly
Le Charivari, founded two years after the victors of the July Revolution of 1930 rein-
stated a limited monarchy and appointed citizen King Louis-Philippe to the throne.
Le Charivari was the most critically outspoken journal in France until its editor, the
writer and cartoonist Charles Philipon, published an image that savagely ridiculed
the reigning monarch and became a popular icon of dissent. The image was called
Les Poires (The Pears), a four-step transformation of the stout, jowled king into a
plump, overripe pear, which, in addition to being a witty visual metaphor, proved
to be an incendiary insult as well, for *le poire* in French slang signifies a simpleton
or dope.

Ralph E. Shikes, author of *The Indignant Eye*, notes that "Many of [Philipon's] fellow artists, like gleeful delinquents, returned to the theme again and again." Indeed, The Pear became so ingrained in the French vernacular that it was a devastating symbolic blow against authority in an era when symbols carried great weight— Louis-Philippe was so threatened by it that he ordered harsh punitive measures against any cartoonists using the image and eventually decreed that The Pear (and, not too long afterward, the entire free press of France) must cease to exist. But the clever Philipon found a loophole, noting that the decree *only* prohibited The Pear from being drawn by an artist's or engraver's hand, leaving typographical representation unscrutinized. In a final act of defiance before the censors squelched free expression almost entirely, Philipon published a fiery editorial against censorship typeset on the cover of *Le Charivari* in the shape of *Les Poires*. This act, though a difficult technical accomplishment, since it was handset in lead type, was well worth the effort for the consternation it caused officialdom.

Philipon's feat was indeed witty and smart, but it was not, however, a new invention. His typographic manipulation had a history and a name: *figured verse*. It is actually traceable back to long before the advent of moveable type, to when the scribes of Ancient Greece gave concrete form to poetic expression. One of the most famous figured verses in English literature appeared in the nineteenth century as "The Mouse's Tail," from *Alice in Wonderland*, in which words form a swirling tail, giving visual emphasis to the character of the mouse. Perhaps the most emblematic example of this genre is Guillaume Apollinaires's poem, "Il Pleut" (It's Raining), from *Calligrammes: Poemes de la Paix et de la Guerre (1913–1916)*, with words that metaphorically fall like rain on a page.

Modern Humor

Other Modernist poets and graphic designers also gave voice to words through what one critic has called "noisy" typography. But Apollinaire coined a more poetic term, *calligramme*, to signify a combination of script, design, and thought, "representing the shortest route which can be taken for expressing a thought in material terms, and for forcing the eye to accept a global view of the written word." His revival of this venerable means of expression provided the perfect tool for Modern functionalists, who preferred machine-made imagery (i.e., realistic drawing). Calligrammes and similar typographic concoctions became the means for progressive artists, writers, and designers to express themselves economically and functionally with the proper Modern materials. Variations on the calligramme, both witty and profane, were created by members of the Futurist, Constructivist, and Dadaist movements in manifestos expressing the goals of their respective cultural revolutions. Indeed, these documents challenged existing artistic canons even as they questioned conventional means of comprehension.

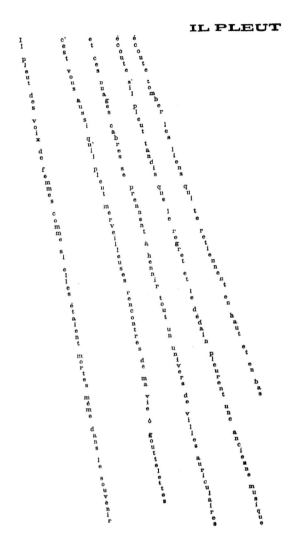

IL PLEUT

"Il Pleut," from Calligrames (1918), by Guillaume Apollinaire.

One of the most radical proponents of this new visual language was F. T. Marinetti, the father of Italian Futurism, who invented the *Parole in Liberta* ("Words in Freedom"), giving sound to typography. As early as 1910, he wrote that to enliven the printed page he would use "three or four inks of different colors on a single page and twenty different typefaces if necessary." His goal was to create a new synthetic means of expression. Moreover, through a visual-verbal assault, he hoped to shock Europe's stagnating intellects into joining the modern world. However, what he and the other European avant-gardists pioneered as a new language was soon adopted and promulgated by commercial and advertising artists as *style*. While the avant-gardists were challenging and perhaps even having serious fun at the expense of convention, the commercial artists appropriated safe and unthreatening aspects of the Modernist visual vocabulary, establishing new design conventions and making the "far-out" accessible to a mass audience. Indeed, in the hands of commercial artists, calligrammes and other concrete typography were effective means of creating mnemonic devices to ensure product identification. Massin wrote that this method "fuses a visual image and a script and gives a tangible quality to the metaphor. It offers a slogan which is made up of words, a concrete presence and an immediate significance so that its power is reinforced to a remarkable degree."

Moderne Humor

The Modern movement rejected antiquated styles. Conversely, the Moderne style—the dominant mode of mass commercial art that ran concurrent with Modernism from the early 1920s to the mid-1930s—enthusiastically embraced them. While the Modernists sought to develop a timeless vocabulary resistant to the erosive effects of fashion, Moderne (or modernistic) designers derived their popular style from a confluence of historical and contemporary influences that was deliberately fashionable and predictably short-lived. Wry, sophisticated humor was key to certain aspects of Modern design, while Moderne design humor was generally less intellectually rigorous. However, since Moderne design drew its inspiration from mass culture and was directed at the mass market, it had to be much more comic in certain respects, for lightheartedness in advertising and publicity was a proven commercial lure. Owing to the limited color palette and type choice of Modern graphic design, especially as practiced under the banners of the Bauhaus and the New Typography, the avant-garde was perceived by some critics as too austere, humorless, and therefore too off-putting to be successful in the marketplace. Modernism was accepted more warmly in Europe than in the United States, where advertising "experts" consistently underestimated public tolerance for new things.

Since Moderne designers did not reject drawing or painting as viable design tools, and because their color palette was rich and typographic variations numerous, the range of graphic materials produced under the modernistic umbrella was usually quite joyful and witty. Much modernistic design was illustrative, and since humor was easier to achieve with illustration than with type alone, Moderne humor must be viewed as ostensibly pictorial.

Excellent examples of this pictorial mode include the posters by the Italian artist Leonetto Cappiello, who was a prolific posterist in France and Italy during the early twentieth century and achieved memorable imagery through his comic, gestural drawings. Cappiello's lettering was bold and straightforward, with his humor usually conveyed through a single figure surrealistically juxtaposed with the object being advertised. An example of this is the human firefly surrounded by light bulbs in his brilliant poster for *Lampe Osmine*. French artist Jean Carlu, another Moderne master, was not as interested in gestural drawing as was Cappiello but nevertheless had a pictorial rather than typographic orientation. His comic images, which advertised a wide range of quotidian products, were based on a synthesis of borrowed Cubist forms into cartoonlike signposts. Carlu's poster for *Dentifrices Gellé Frères* uses stylish lettering to identify the product, but the focus is on the discordant shapes forming the comic head and shadow. The target is a spotlight on the teeth (which A. Tollmer, a 1930s design critic, called "the graphic dart"). This poster is also clever on another level, for rather than showing a package, as was the convention of the day, Carlu created a semiabstract, comic trademark that was effectively applied to other selling materials.

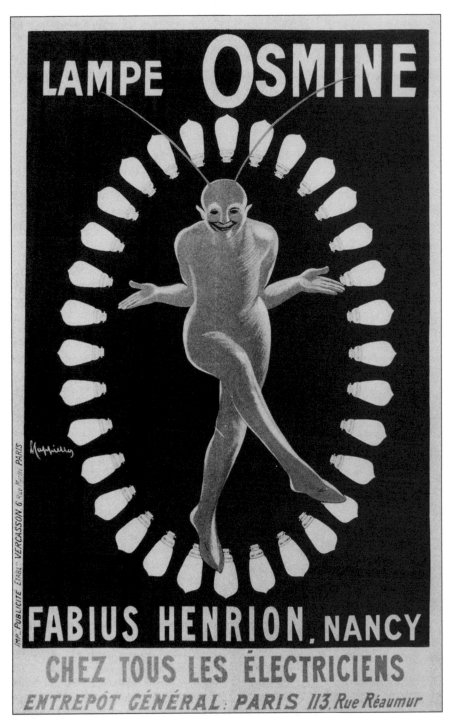

Lampe Osmine *advertising poster by Leonetto Cappiello (1920).*

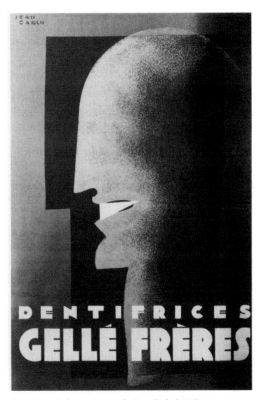

Dentifrices Gellé Frères *poster by Jean Carlu (1927).*

Iconic trademarks by Karl Schulpig (1919–1924).

Carlu was a master but not, however, the originator of this method of pictographic, humorous design. Before him, in the 1910s and 1920s, many German trademark designers, most notably Karl Schulpig, were cleverly playing with stark geometries with the goal of changing logo and trademark imagery from the intricate heraldic marks of the previous century to simplified and witty graphic pictograms. This change was necessary because business dominance was shifting—small, family-run concerns were increasingly giving way to large, shareholder-owned corporations—and the venerable means of identification were quickly becoming obsolete in this new business culture. Schulpig developed marks and posters that offered a more abstract approach, but never so confounding as to be incomprehensible (like some of today's marks). Many of these images were like puzzles, which, when deciphered, became unforgettable. One exemplary mark designed by John Heartfield for the Malik-Verlag, a German socialist publishing company, was a pictogram of a comic robot

Malik-Verlag logo by John Heartfield (1918). formed by the sans serif letters M A L I K.

13

Illustration versus Design

Not all pictorial humor is design humor. While many forms of illustration and cartoon are used in concert with type, only some of these relationships are actually driven by design. Cappiello's imagery was definitely illustrative, but the drawings in his posters were not used to tell a narrative story, but rather as mnemonic symbols (which is my simple definition of "illustrative"). Similarly, Carlu was not making narrative illustration, but rather a pictorial symbology that developed from design requisites.

Shown here are examples of purely humorous illustration on the covers of *Harper's Weekly*, *Satire*, *Liberty*, and the *Saturday Evening Post* magazines, in which no attempt is made to unify the typographic elements with the artwork. Each piece of art is a narrative, telling a story by freezing a moment of time into a vignette or tableau. These images may be witty or even satiric, but they are not examples of design humor. Conversely, the artwork and lettering for the cover of *Vanity Fair*, rendered by Fortunato Depero, is seamlessly intertwined, like a miniposter. The intent of the cover is not to tell a story, but to express a feeling about New York wealth and privilage in a witty manner. And on page 16 are two billboards (c. 1938), in which comic characterizations are in concert with amusing lettering. While these can be considered design humor, each represents a more slapstick approach than, say, the posters by Cappiello, Carlu, or Agha.

Harpers Weekly *(1901)* and Satire *(1911) featured witty cartoons and illustrations on the covers.*

Liberty *(1940) and the* Saturday Evening Post *(1959) relied on humorous paintings and comic vignettes to attract readers.*

The Vanity Fair *(1931) cover by Fortunato Depero uses characters based on comic cubistic forms.*

The Talon Fasteners character (c. 1932) is built around exaggerated geometries.

The chefs on the A&P Bread billboard (c. 1935) prefigure the cuddly Pillsbury Doughboy.

Postwar Humor

A schism of varying degrees has existed between illustrator and designer ever since the advent of commercial printing, which allowed the artist to make artwork in a virtual vacuum, ignorant of how the work would be used in a layout. But at no time was the schism more profound than during the post–World War II era, when descendants of the Modern movement in Europe and the United States fervently rejected drawn or painted illustration in favor of more "objective" or "rational" media, such as photography and photomontage. The direct descendants of the Bauhaus developed the Swiss Style, a rather systematic, functional design approach based on a less-is-more philosophy, which was perceived by its critics as totally devoid of humor. Of course, nothing can be so black and white, and while Swiss design is definitely austere, it is not completely humorless. Indeed, Josef Müller-Brockman's much-reproduced poster protesting noise pollution is an economical form but an acerbic and bittersweet message.

Swiss design reflected the temperament of the Swiss nation during the postwar years, and also perpetuated the stereotype of their squeaky-clean and well-ordered society. But more importantly, Swiss graphic design was a profound influence on designers elsewhere in the industrialized world, who were beginning to administer to the identity needs of the emerging multinational corporations requiring manageable, uniform design systems. In America, however, small pockets of rebellion grew in response to rationalist trends perceived as cold and humorless. Pushpin Studios, founded in 1954 by the illustrators Seymour Chwast, Milton Glaser, Reynold Ruffins, and Edward Sorel, became the most recognized and influential of these rebels. Pushpin was also the progenitor of a new

American eclecticism noted for returning illustration back to the design process. Pushpin developed a distinctive, decidedly humorous pictorial vocabulary by reviving and synthesizing historical European graphic styles and American vernacular art, like the comics, into a cacophony of type and imagery. Humor in all forms—from jest to pun to parody—was key to the Pushpin style. And its inventive house organ, *The Pushpin Monthly Graphic*, was a proving ground for its various members' graphic humor. Fortunately, Pushpin's clients were primarily in the entertainment, publishing, and culture fields, which tended to prefer to be represented by humor.

Seymour Chwast's shaky drawn line is inherently funny.

Late Modern Humor

Graphic design came of age during the 1950s, when the field was no longer called commercial art, but "art for commerce"—a fine but very significant distinction that implies a higher lever of collaboration between artist and business. The leading practitioners were not anonymous craftspersons but respected communicators, some with distinctive personal styles, others with notable philosophies, and a few even holding revolutionary ideas in the tradition of the European avant-gardes. Paul Rand, a very early exponent of progressive design in the United States, made his mark in advertising during the late 1930s through his emphasis on quite playful, visual solutions instead of the ubiquitous copy-driven ads. In the 1950s, he made even more signif-

icant inroads into the infant field of corporate communications, combining the best of the Swiss systematic design with his personal passion for play. Rand instinctively imbued his book jackets, posters, and even children's books with wry humor to enhance both eye appeal

Logos by Paul Rand for Westinghouse (1960) and UPS (1961), noted for their comic twists.

and meaning, and believed firmly that even corporate design could benefit from play. His most visible corporate logos and trademarks are witty visual puns. For example, the logo for Westinghouse, a *W*, is an electrical schematic, while the one for UPS is an heraldic shield with a gift box as a crown.

During the late 1950s, typeplay evolved from the anarchic Dada and Futurist manifestations into more deliberate communications. Bradbury Thompson, who devoted an entire 1949 issue of *Westvaco Inspirations* (the paper company's influential promotional magazine to the subject of type as metaphor, was himself a skilled master of this typographic art. Through witty layouts in which type was used to mimic sound, Thompson proved that type was an extraordinarily versatile expressive tool.

If Thompson helped emancipate hot type from the shackles of the chase, Herb Lubalin gave type its many voices, some of them comedic.

Bradbury Thompson's cover of Mademoiselle *pays homage to René Magritte.*

With the rebus in mind, Lubalin made words and images read together as single entities in compositions that were at once witty and true. But his really important, groundbreaking work came with the advent of the phototypositor, for he experimented with such close settings and contorted juxtapositions that he became known as the "master of smashed type." By tightening, touching, and overlapping letterforms, he forced a radical break from the standards that had governed typesetting for ages. At the same time, he tamed the more anarchic manifestations of the avant-garde into an *au courant* typographic language, at once playful and accessible.

Bradbury Thompson makes letters into an African mask.

Prefiguring sound-bite mania, but concurrent with television's rise in popularity during the early 1960s, the brightest American advertising art directors, in collaboration with their creative team partners, created a genre of word-image advertising notable for its straightforward design, matter-of-fact image (usually photographic), and sophisticated wit. Influenced by television, the best print campaign competed successfully with the tube for memorability. Indeed, three campaigns are still unforgettable after almost three decades, because their ideas were so ingenious and the design so innovative that they continue to defy quibble and qualm: George Lois's Wolfschmidt's Vodka campaign, in which tasty fruit and vegetable additives converse smartly with tasteless alcohol; Helmut Krone's Volkswagen campaign, the first time an advertiser revealed its own faults in public; and William Taubin

The "Mother and Child" logo by Herb Lubalin is the quintessential visual pun.

"Pure, innocent water. What a setup."

"Wolfschmidt, I wouldn't do this with any other vodka. You've got taste."

"Can you squeeze me in?"

"Crazy Water." (Water never tasted this good before.)

For the Wolfschmidts vodka campaign, George Lois gave inanimate objects comic life by giving them voices.

Levy's Rye Bread campaign, in which various members of New York's ethnic melting pot declared on large subway posters that "You don't have to be Jewish to love Levy's." In addition, Lou Dorfsman, design director for CBS, was writing and designing brilliantly witty advertising during this period. Though well-crafted words are the keys to the success of these ads, memorability is based on the sum of their parts—text, image and typography—as well as on their confident and at times self-effacing humor.

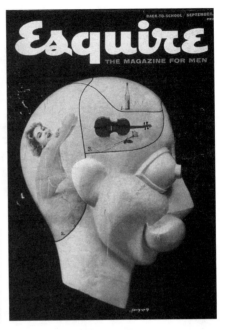

William Taubin's ironic word- and picture-play for Levy's.

Henry Wolf's sexy phrenology for Esquire.

Post-Modern Humor

The term Post-Modern, when applied to graphic design, is an attitude, not a style, associated with the time period from the mid-1970s to the present. Literally, *Post-Modernism* is historiographic nomenclature for the ethic that follows Modernism. Philosophically, it describes a reassessment and revival throughout art and design of historical and vernacular styles and materials formerly rejected by Modernism and outmoded by fashion. In architecture and literature, Post-Modernism, simply stated, is an analytical process of "deconstructing" a particular work in order to discover its formal origins; in graphic design, however, the term is merely a convenient catchall for a broad range of contemporary design applications, none of them directly related to each other by one dominant ethic. Post-Modern graphic design is neither a movement with a moral mission nor a school with shared beliefs, but rather a number of vaguely linked aesthetics. When the history of the period from the mid-1970s to the 1990s is codified, it will include an array of computer, vernacular, historicist, decorative, and informational designers who might superficially share similar color preferences or borrow from the same big closet of revivals—some of the design from this period may look like it was cryogenically preserved back in the 1930s, while other pieces will seem to have returned from the twenty-fifth century. But more important than these minor shared attributes, the most significant characteristic to emerge from Post-Modernism is a profound sense of play and humor.

Punk magazine cover comic by Bobby London.

The Post-Modern play ethic began during the postpsychedelic era in the early 1970s with the short-lived, youth-inspired design language called Punk. Punk was reheated Dada without the content, and souped-up 1960s pop without the Vietnam War as an anchor for moral indignation. Punk, which began in England as a musical trend and spread as a design style throughout Europe and the United States in publications like *Slash*, *New York Rocker*, and, predictably, *Punk*, was about kids coming of age—cynical, sarcastic, angry, and anarchic kids. Punk's design humor was acerbic but not necessarily strident, raucous but not really intelligent. It was a slap-and-paste ethic. Formalism be damned, expression was supreme. Punk's jugular humor wore thin, as did the "movement" itself, which quickly lost steam and was assimilated into the mainstream within a few years of its initial surge of energy.

Replacing Punk was New Wave, or what the cartoonist Gary Panter calls "sanitized punk." New Wave took the primitive Punk visual utterances and transformed them into visual language, with syntax and grammar. The vocabulary was comprised of soothing colors, a plethora of geometric dingbats and ornaments, and humorous imagery often borrowed from old commercial-arts manuals. New Wave designers made it possible to apply Punk to mainstream advertising, the same way Moderne designers had borrowed aspects of Cubism for commercial purposes decades earlier.

If Punk contributed anything to the practice of graphic design, it was the idea that somehow everything was possible—rules didn't matter. Of course, not all designers (or clients, for that matter) are comfortable with such freedom, but that didn't inhibit young designers in the 1980s from experimenting, even if it meant reinventing the wheel.

If American graphic design came of age in the late 1950s, it was primarily in New York, Chicago and Los Angeles, the three centers of "enlightened" business and design savvy. In the 1980s, graphic design entered middle age by expanding into regions of the United States where designers had never flourished before. Many of these areas developed somewhat indigenous or regional styles owing to the influence of one or two leading stylists and the kinds of businesses being serviced. In San Francisco, Michael Vanderbyl and Michael Manwaring were influenced by contemporary pop culture (including San Francisco's psychedelic legacy), Post-Modern architecture, and the comic furniture of Milan's Memphis group. Sharing common passions, their work was a synthesis of these contemporary ideas into a distinctive vocabulary of lighthearted New Wave forms underscored by serious visual punning. In Dallas, Woody Pirtle, who was influenced by Pushpin Studios, developed an illustrative design method that was founded on visual puns and witty juxtapositions of content. And in Minneapolis, The Duffy Group exemplified Midwest New Wave styling (in a similar manner to the early work of Pushpin Studios) and a new "vernacular" humor using cuts from 1920s and 1930 printer's manuals. Apparently spell-

Stuff magazine's abstract cover design exudes whimsy.

I WaNNA STeaL HOME I waNNa BReaK THe BaCKBoaRD I WANNA DOWNSHIFT TO PaSS I WaNNA Be IN THE PaINT I WaNNA PLaY TO WIN I WaNNA FaT CONTRaCT I WaNNA SHOOT FROM THRee I WaNNa ReDLINE I WaNNa **BE YOUNG** I WaNNa STOP A SLaP SHOT I WaNNA DaNCE IN THE eND ZONE I WaNNA SINK ONe aT THE BuZZeR I WaNNA JOG THe BaSeS I WaNNA RETIRE IN COOPeRSTOWN I WaNNa DROP IN AT WAIMeA I WaNNa Be IN THe POLe POSITION I WaNNA DIG IN MY CLeaTS I WaNNa BeND THE RIM I WaNNa INTeRCePT THE BOMB I WaNNa **HAVE FUN** I WaNNa POP THe CLUTCH I WaNNa GO THE DISTaNCE I WaNNA TRUCK FULL OF TROPHIES I WaNNa WeaR THE RING I WaNNa Be THe MVP I WaNNA I WaNNA TKO I WaNNa CRACK aN ALUMINUM BaT I WaNNa Be A SHOWSTOPPeR I WaNNa Be A CROWD PLeaSeR I WaNNa DRINK PEPSI

David Carson transformed mere type into mere Pepsi.

bound by that innocent, yet kitschy, period of commercial art, Charles Spencer Anderson created a vocabulary based on silly but curiously compelling stock images, manipulating them ever so slightly and printing them in contemporary colors.

M&Co, a progressive New York firm founded by the late Tibor and Maira Kalman and currently operated by the latter, also built its early studio personality on a rehabilitation of old printing forms. But unlike Anderson's quite stylized work, M&Co used vernacular forms in contrast to (and perhaps as a satire of) the overly sophisticated, indeed superficially decorative trends underscoring American graphic communications. Anderson's approach is rooted in the pleasure that results from playing with these anomalous forms, while M&Co believe that studying vernacular art provides a method for breaking through the clichés that hamper interesting communication and constrict intelligent humor.

The Duffy Group transformed old commercial art into a new style.

Tibor Kalman used "vernacular" images as an ironic critique of slick graphic design.

Even in the Post-Modern era, where a simple evocation of the past seems enough to make design humorous, not all humor is based on common nostalgic visual cues. Humor's determinants are complex and fluid, and actively resist categorization.

Digital Age Humor

Since the abrupt end of Post-Modernism in the late Nineties, graphic design is bereft of viable rubrics with which to label contemporary forms and styles. Generally speaking, this has been an eclectic period during which innovation has more or less taken a back seat to reaction. It has been a time when distressed, hyperactive, and otherwise convention-slaying typography has often been more a knee-jerk reaction to the sobriety of Modernism and the superfluities of the Post-Modernism eras than an new movement that has embraced original ideas. One might say that a large proportion of the graphic design produced during the cur-rent *fin de siecle* has been a joke. This is not to suggest that graphic design is entirely facetious, but since the relevance of graphic design as a communications field has been in question with relation to other mass media forms, designers may not be as serious as they once were. Which is not a criticism but an observation that designers now have a curious license to be less solemn about their work. Although humor has been significant during all the eras of design discussed in this chapter, the Digital Age is typified by frivolity that has not been experienced since the days of Dada.

Digital media have made it possible for designers to cavort in ways that were unthinkable because they were not doable prior to the advent of the personal computer. Today, designers are able to animate what was once static, amplify what was once silent, and introduce multiple dimensions to what was once two-dimen-sional. Some of these creations are manifest as a new period style as typified by multiple layers of visual matter, but much of today's output is unique unto itself—often, in fact the meanderings of a designer's distinct persona. The Digital Age has spawned many individuals hungry for individuality, and humor has proven, as always, a good means of attracting attention. Modernist humor was simply a result of good design, not its goal; but for the Digital Age-ist, making humor is often the problem, the solution, and the be-all-end-all.

Before the computer (B.C.) the graphic designer was an organizer, aesthetic advi-sor, and conceptualist mostly in the print medium. Now, the graphic designer has the power to be more in many media. Today the designer is an entertainer, and there are few things more entertaining than humor. Making design (in the broadest sense of the word, which involves the confluence of letter, image, and form) that will spark an audience to laugh is as important as creating superb typography. With current dig-ital authoring tools—Photoshop, Flash, and Final Cut-Pro, for example—the designer is more equipped than ever to produce entertainment for both pleasure and edification—often both.

Design for pleasure is easy to describe. It is anything that makes the communication experience—the conveyance of information—enjoyable. Humor is the spark that ignites the pleasure center of the brain. If one laughs, one enjoys, and when one enjoys, one must experience happiness. Design for edification is not necessarily distinct from pleasure, but being edified is usually separate from pure pleasure. Edification involves being informed—awareness is the fruit—and serious information on political, social, and cultural issues is usually a pill best administered with a witty coating. When, for example, the Enron scandal hit the proverbial fan in winter 2002, visual humorists attacked the issue through graphic satire. The enormity of the corruption and the number of innocent people who were hurt by corporate greed made it difficult to exercise humor, and therefore all the more important. The reaction of visual commentators helped make the complexities of the event more concrete. And no tool was more useful than the Enron logo, which when Paul Rand designed it in 1996 could never be considered an infamous mark. Its tilting *E*, a metaphor for the pipelines that the company administered, was Rand's characteristic plaything. He always injected mild covert wit into everything he designed, but now that tilt is indicative of a corporation that jilted its employees and screwed the nation. By 2002 the Enron logo had become such an emblem of infamy that visual humorists were using it as a touchstone for fast wit and serious commentary. Even a Web site that called for an "Enron Logo Contest," piqued such imagination that scores of designers made variations that included a severed *E* as middle finger and the *E* as broken pipelines spewing waste onto the land.

The Enron logo became a symbol of malfeasance.

Digital Age humor is really no different from most other periods, only the delivery has changed and so have the practitioners. With the computer a designer need not be a "designer" to produce "sophisticated" graphic wit—or cheap shots, for that matter. During the 2000 election, when Al Gore and George W. Bush duked it out in Florida for the few contested votes, the Internet was a swarm of GIFFs, TIFFs, JPEGs, and PDFs that lampooned the presumptive Dubya by casting aspersions on his character, intelligence, and physiognomy. Most of these gags were not created by "professional" designers, yet they worked perfectly well as ad hoc digital flyers. The message was conveyed, the form was acceptable, and the humor was sharp. In the Digital Age anyone can design, and that's no joke. It's ironic that graphic design was for so long such an unknown profession, and then with the advent of the digital bust, it's become so well-known that anyone can do it, but I digress.

Speaking of irony, certain pundits have dubbed the mid-Eighties and Nineties "The Age of Irony," the nothing-is-sacred era, the ripe for sarcasm decades, the Comedy Central epoch. It is what commentator Kurt Andersen has referred to as "a certain kind of easy, preening, nihilistic posture." Immediately after the tragedy of 9/11, irony was on the chopping block. *Time* magazine, one of the least ironic journals around, declared that, "One good thing could come from this horror—the end of the age of irony." But without irony, what is humor? Irony has been the mainstay of satire, the knife that cuts through the sanctimony of hypocritical society. Of course, the old saying, "There is a place for everything [read as humor] and everything in its place," certainly applies to tragedies as devastating as holocaust, genocide, and terrorist murder, but horror requires perspective. Humor, indeed irony, is not a drug that blocks pain, though it aids in prioritizing emotion. After 9/11 the immediate response by many designers was to create posters, symbols, and other graphics to commemorate victims, exhibit patriotism, or call citizens to arms. Some of the visual puns involved were clever, though most rested on tried and true national clichés designed to instill comfort and recognition. For a moment irony was lost. But as Kurt Andersen noted, "It turns out there is a half-life to trauma."

Post-Traumatic-Stress Humor

The satirical newspaper and Web site *The Onion*, known for its ironic tabloid social jibes, jumped headlong into the post-9/11 fray without compromising its pre-9/11 mission. It carries forward the legacy of Fifties *Mad*, Sixties *National Lampoon*, and Eighties *Spy* with its spot-on, nerve-touching social and political spoofs, but in the wake of tragedy it was even more compelling, dealing with high-stakes realities such as its mock news story about homeland security, headlined "'Expect Delays' Signs Placed Randomly Throughout Nation." *The Onion* is design humor in its broadest definition. The publication and Web site employ a transparently emblematic format—in other words, it functions as what it is—a mock tabloid that enables the material to be conveyed without distraction or deflection.

Well before 9/11, George W. Bush and the conservative congressional agenda provided stimulus for visual and verbal satirists. In addition, other social follies in the ferment were ready for critical attacks, notably the controversy surrounding meetings of the World Trade Organization. *Adbusters* magazine, the bible of the anti-brand and "No-Logo" movement, had been wittily designed to give an aura of sophistication while much of its visual content was dedicated to transforming well-known logos, trademarks, and advertisements into satires against environmental and cultural waste-makers. However, 9/11 marked a moment of reevaluation both for its contributors and audience. How could any protest, especially humorous protest, be mounted against world trade after is foremost symbol had been the target of such a deadly terrorist attack. Nonetheless, despite critics who called for a moratorium on critical wit,

Robbie Conal captures the warts and all of American political "heroes."

Adbusters did not demur and used satire as one of its weapons in a cause it believed still had relevance. *Adbusters* further sponsored a billboard on Times Square that slyly used the American flag, but instead of stars appeared the logos of the nation's leading corporations. Similarly, artist-designers known for their respective pre-9/11 graphic assaults on political and social bêtes noires found that they could not be silent for long. Robbie Conal is the preeminent American poster sniper; Shawn Wolfe is the leading critic of brand-fetishism. Both use their respective media and irony to critique issues and individuals. Conal's "Homeland" poster (see page 168) was a frontal jab against government rhetoric that he believed was an excuse for draconian legal measures. Wolfe has wrestled with commodification of the soul to planned obsolescence. His work repeatedly teases what he calls "consumer hoodoo" as found in the worlds of fashion and style through a parodying of conventional methods of communication.

Throughout the twentieth century, irony has been a response to staggering historical developments, to World Wars I and II, and the threat of World War III. "At times like these," states Kurt Andersen, "wisdom and well-crafted wisecracking can go hand-in-hand." The function of design humor in times of strife have a curative and cautionary result. Humor may cover but also exposes. It is more than a salve applied to a wound—it is a way to uncover the anxieties that mount in the wake of hardship. This is has been a time when humor in general, and graphic wit very directly, have served a variety of purposes, but none greater than to entertain and edify.

Having now explored the various forms graphic wit and design humor have taken since prehistory, the following chapters deliver on this book's intent: how graphic wit and design humor have evolved in America in recent years.

Shawn Wolfe's Panic Now campaign promotes a useless appliance.

Amusing
things just stick
in people's heads
a little better.
And that's certainly
a goal
when you're out to
create
effective
communication.

Alex Isley

The use of **humor** allows corporate clients to **maximize** their **synergistic paradigms** in regard to **corporate communications.**

Charles Spencer Anderson

Wit is the SUGAR that precedes the medicine.

Mark Fox

Chapter

Play at Work

Civilization and Its Malcontents

Play is the work of children. Yet children do not merely busy themselves with play-things, but rather learn invaluable lessons and relationships through processes of dis-covery inherent in their play. In its purest form, play is joy unrefined, free of con-straint. Furthermore, play is the fuel of creativity. Romantically speaking, play is primitivism, because it is not derivative of style or fashion. Since primitivism allows for honest expression, and since children are indeed primitive before they become "civilized," it is no wonder that artists like Paul Klee, Joan Miro, and Saul Steinberg quote their children's imagery as a means of expressing their own primal natures. Neither is it surprising that Abstract Expressionist painting has been compared to the work of children, for despite the grandiloquent art historical theories, many abstract artists in the late 1940s attempted to rediscover those realms of play that society had deemed so unsuitable for responsible adults. "Play so that you may be serious," advised Aristotle. "Play freely so that your mind is a welcome home for every new dis-covery," said a sixth grade art teacher.

Play is a noble activity. Yet in addition to noble play, there is also mischievous play. Though the two should not necessarily be mutually exclusive, sometimes they are direct opposites. While noble play is cherished abandon, mischief is synonymous with premeditated irresponsibility. But mischief can also be more intense play—think about Shakespeare's Puck in A *Midsummer Night's Dream*, who may be devilish but not Satanic, for he is the embodiment of eternal youth. An inveterate prankster, Puck is forever disrupting the status quo, not for the simple pleasure of wreaking havoc but rather as a comic reminder that life should be wonderfully spirited, not lifelessly constricted. Puck's distant cousin Peter Pan is the prince of pranks, whose entire existence is forever linked to children's imaginations and their unwillingness to grow up. What's wrong with keeping at least some of the attributes of youth alive, asks Oscar Wilde in *The Picture of Dorian Grey*: "Youth smiles without any reason. It is one of its chiefest charms." What some might call mischief is actually just an attempt to sustain youthful vigor. Whatever the rationale, a certain amount of mischief is necessary for the creative process to begin and continue.

Art and design are to a certain extent driven by mischief. Indeed, the world expects it, and expects to complain about it too. If we look at certain art as mischief in the making, then some of the aesthetic blunders and conceptual stupidities of the contemporary East Village art scene are more palatable. Tracing mischief in art history, one might conclude in hindsight that some of the most well-known blunders and folly were brilliantly rightheaded. For example, as a respite from the rigors of his official commissions, Leonardo da Vinci drew distorted, vexing portraits of noble and common people which were considered beyond the ken of his patrons and inconsistent with artistic convention. Likewise, the sculptor Bernini took certain liberties with the visages of Vatican clerics in mildly "charged" portraits that seemed trivial and beneath his talent, given the artistic standards of his era. But both of these masters' "playthings" became the historical basis for the "serious" art of caricature. Young Renaissance painters in training engaged in harmless mischief when they painted over academic portraits and landscapes with flies and other crawling creatures, as if in a trompe l'oeil, rendered in perfect detail. These pranks provided a reference point for subsequent visual satirists who developed a truly critical art. And jumping into the more recent past, during the early 1920s the Dadaists raised artistic mischief to a high art through images that at once ridiculed the church, army, and government of a morally decaying Germany and created a new expressive visual language based on a menu of aesthetically unacceptable forms. The role of mischief is therefore not to be underestimated.

Play is necessary to the design process because unless a designer is working within a rigid design system that prohibits all variants, exploration is an integral part of all initial problem solving. When a new toy called *Colorforms* was introduced in 1930, with its sheets of brightly colored geometric shapes that adhered to a shiny black board without glue or tape, it became a huge commercial success despite the fact that it was neither a talking doll nor a mechanical toy. Children were fascinated by the countless pictorial variations that were possible with a finite number of geometric shapes. Indeed, many adults were hooked on it too, because it allowed for all kinds of random constructions, like a huge doodle. Colorforms is therefore an appropriate metaphor for the early stage of the graphic design process, which is inherently limited yet curiously limitless. The act of playing with Colorforms is a metaphor for designing, since the image potential is wide ranging—realistic or abstract, witty or serious, traditional or innovative—just like the range of design solutions in the real world. The first Colorforms instruction manual showed some of the possibilities, including abstract pictures, presumably made by children, that were strikingly similar to Russian Suprematist and Dutch Neo-Plasticist Paintings, as well as the more predictable narrative pictures of girls and boys, ships and cars, and so on. (Incidentally, in 1959 Paul Rand redesigned the Colorforms trademark, using the toy's own available shapes, thereby blending abstract and realistic characteristics into one pictogram.)

Character trademark for Colorforms, by Paul Rand

The creative potential offered by Colorforms is proscribed not by the limited number of pieces, shapes, and colors but by the child's imagination and skill. If the child's mind is boundless, then so is the game; if the child is constrained by certain limits, then the game has its limits too. To a great extent, this same equation defines the practice of graphic design.

Law and Order

As important as play is to problem solving, graphic design is defined by the imposition of certain limitations and rules, usually imposed by the client, vendor, or printer—every designer must work from a brief and conform to a budget. These real-world determinants distinguish a child at play from a graphic designer at work. These constraints, however, must be seen as a distinct advantage. In A *Designer's Art*, Paul Rand notes in his chapter on "Design and the Play Instinct" that while the ultimate success of a designer's work depends on his or her natural talents, the problem in design education comes from how to arouse curiosity and stimulate creativity. Rand concludes that limitless freedom is counterproductive and not as useful as the imposition of a set of rules against which the designer can push the recognized limits. Total freedom curiously fosters inertia, because without rules, there can be no motivation to *break* rules. By extension, broken rules often (but not always) imply innovative solutions. Without structure, play becomes energy draining rather than intellectually sustaining.

Graphic design play also differs from child's play in terms of results. This may seem obvious or implicit, but distinguishing the two types of play in nevertheless worth repeating: The child's fingerpainting or collage will be adored by a loving parent no matter what it looks like, while a graphic designer's presentation will be intensely scrutinized by the client. From child's play come randomness; from adult play comes concept. Random imagery is an end in itself, while concept is the basis for a solution, which translates into visual communication. Humor may be born out of randomness, or even chaos, but humorous design solutions as exemplified in this book must be planned and purposeful.

That designers should be endowed with a play instinct is not surprising—otherwise, why would anyone spend days and nights pushing type and pictures around on sheets of paper or computer screens: That design play must be *controlled*, however, is the critical aspect of creativity—anyone can play with visual or graphic elements, but only a graphic designer can make them into meaningful communication. A designer must know when to play and when to stop. A designer must intuit how far play can be pushed before the fruits of instinct need to be mediated by an overriding logic. Play thus becomes the first step in a process that ultimately involves quick decision making, in addition to astute knowledge of and keen expertise with tools and materials.

Fun Is Not Always Funny

While not all play is humorous, play is definitely the first stage in achieving graphic wit and design humor. Unless a designer can literally project his or her mental picture of a humorous idea onto a page or object with perfect fidelity, then playing with graphic elements until the right relationships emerge is indispensable for achieving a humorous result. While there are no surefire formulae governing wit or humor—in fact, the most successful humor, though rooted in intelligence, is usually serendipitous—there exist some accepted formal tools that designers must use to create a nurturing environment for the humorous idea. Some of these devices are obvious (and even clichéd), while others are not.

Veteran vaudevillians used to say that performers could ensure laughter if they took pratfalls, accepted pies in the face, insulted "dames," or simply berated their audiences. (Given the dubious success of Andrew Dice Clay, the sexist-antagonist principle is still disappointingly valid.) Circus clowns have a virtual catalog of visual gags and tricks guaranteed to "make 'em role in da aisles every time." And in *Enjoyment of Laughter*, Max Eastman acts as a self-appointed lawgiver to the would-be joke teller in his "Nine Commandments of Comic Arts":

1. Be interesting.
2. Be unimpassioned.
3. Be effortless.
4. Remember the difference between cracking practical jokes and conveying ludicrous impressions.
5. Be plausible.
6. Be sudden.
7. Be neat.
8. Be right with your timing.
9. Give good measure of serious satisfaction.

Are there equivalencies in the graphic arts? Being neat has never been an important stipulation (neither, for that matter, has legibility), and one might also argue against being too unimpassioned, but some of the other tenets are applicable to graphic design. There are scores of manuals and guides authored by self-styled comedians telling would-be cartoonists and illustrators how to draw funny pictures, and neophyte graphic designers what hilarious novelty typography to use. Printers used to keep reference books with cartoony stock cuts, which any client with a taste for the silly could buy to add the touch of wit to an advertisement or brochure. Without exception, these guides offered a diet of clichés and stereotypes—in fact, reusable printer's cuts were officially called "clichés." Yet smart design humor cannot be achieved by following blueprints of any kind. Play is not a formulaic activity, and mimicry will not ensure a successful result. Perhaps only by example can designers be exposed to what works and what does not. And even then, what works for one design problem might not for another.

With this in mind, the following sections are not intended to bless the reader with an acute prowess in matters witty and humorous, but rather to explore the formal concern common to all graphic design with an eye to how distortion, juxtaposition, repetition, transformation, scale, and shape are manipulated for witty or humorous ends. The material used as examples ranges from subtle to hilarious, from lighthearted to acerbic.

Distortion

In this era of couch-potato home-entertainment systems, the great old traveling carnivals, like the ones featured in the classic film noirs *Nightmare Alley* and *Gun Crazy*, with freakish sideshows and other odd attractions, have all but disappeared. But for those who have a lust for bizarre amusements (as well as good clean fun and games), there remain the county agricultural fairs. These annual celebrations of beef and pork on the hoof are probably the last places in America where one can experience real carnival midways and funhouses, and among the last places to experience the wonderful related attractions. One of the classics is the distortion mirror that stretches and expands a reflection as if it were saltwater taffy. Of all the carnival attractions, the distortion mirror is the most inherently funny, because in stretching and contorting the human form, we see ourselves at our most absurd. No wonder distortion is one of the most common elements in visual humor.

Chip Kidd's book jacket for *Slam* does not offer the reader a vivid picture of this novel about a convicted tax evader who land a job as a caretaker for the estate of a rich old woman who left her fortune to twenty-three cats (and, given that premise, what could?), but does evoke a sense of the bizarre. By anamorphically distorting stock photographs, cropping, skewing, and printing them in loud colors, Kidd's dis-

This book jacket by Chip Kidd uses distortion and dislocation.

Promo by Charles Spencer Anderson, based on stretching and transposition.

This poster illustrated by Mark Frederickson overly exaggerates the anatomy.

embodied heads are reminiscent of the abstract forms made by torn posters on bill postings. And photos are not the only distorted elements of this composition—the title lettering appears to be enlarged well above its original setting, making the typeface unrecognizable as any standard face, which adds to the sense that this design represents many disconnected threads.

If Kidd's distortion produces an abstraction intended to beguile, then Charles Spencer Anderson's comparatively slight distortion of the waiter on the French Paper promotion is intended to personalize an otherwise anonymous rendering borrowed from a 1930s matchbook company sample book. Rather than using it as it is, Anderson exaggerates, and thereby caricatures, the stock cut for the purpose of using nostalgia a commentary.

Mark Frederickson's rendering for The 25th Bird Calling Contest is distortion with a vengeance. His perfect airbrush painting of the birdcaller, with a Mick Jagger–like mouth opened to extremes that the human jawbone would not tolerate, is the focal point of a piece that is made even more humorous by the idea that this feathered man has just been born, having smashed through a bird's egg.

Juxtaposition

All design, graphic or otherwise, is a process of juxtapositioning. A designer must intuitively know where and how to place the operative elements to produce the optimum result. This involves juxtaposing harmonious or discordant images, objects, and letterforms, with no steadfast rules so long as the result is effective. For a massive antinuclear rally held in New York City in 1982, Roger Black designed a simple placard, which said *NO!* in foot-high gothic capitals sitting atop a photo/silk screen of a freshly exploded atomic mushroom cloud. The meaning of this juxtaposition is clear: no more nuclear tests, and *never* a nuclear war. This is not a funny image, per se; it is, however, at once a good example of graphic shorthand, and how juxtapositioning works.

The placard is also a kind of rebus, which is a visual puzzle consisting of pictures of objects, signs, and letter, which, when read together, reveal a sentence, phrase, or message. Much graphic humor turns on the ability of the viewer to decipher, read, and understand a graphic message like Black's "NO!" or Tom Bonauro's somewhat more enigmatic "Scream," for an art exhibition in which he and other like-minded thinkers took part. In this picture puzzle, Bonauro juxtaposed a ghosted photograph of a screaming man, a parodistic version of Munch's *The Scream* without the screaming figure, and the word SCREAM in condensed sans serif type. The game humorously tests the viewer's perceptual ability to fill in the missing piece of the Munch icon. Bonauro extends the boundary of the rebus even further in his brochure for P. Inks. L.A., a rather odd, yet mnemonic, name for a color transfer service. Though the symbolism in ambiguous, the juxtaposition of the logo dropped out of a stark black band next to an enlarged, halftoned 1950s stock photograph printed in blue, with a smaller iconic cut of shaking hands in the foreground, wittily implies that not only does this firm work efficiently with its clients but that it has a sense of humor and therefore pride in what it does. Are we reading too much into this? Perhaps, but such is the demand of Post-Modern design humor.

Roger Black's big NO is proportionally larger than the Big Blast.

Tom Bonauro's design juxtaposes disparate images just like a rebus.

Richard Turtletaub jars the eye with tiny graphic icons.

Given the Post-Modern sensibility, Richard Turtletaub's poster for the AIGA's "Insides/Outsides" show borrows disparate visual references, to create a somewhat surreal rebus, with symbols that suggest the title (and focus) of this show concerned with complete publication design. The details of a naked Venus cleverly fits into a quadrant of the fully clothed model (a 1940s stock shot), rather obviously underscoring the insides/outsides theme. A similar effect is achieved by the cross-section of the nautilus shell, the empty picture frame, and the x-ray of a man's head. Although other references in the poster are more obscure, the overall rebuslike effect is quite successful at conveying the message.

On a more obvious footing, juxtaposition works to enhance visual impact as well as meaning in Paul Scher's design for the cover of *Universal Rhythm*. Here illustrator David Wilcox painted over a dozen stylized men's and women's shoes lined up in a row. The shoes are charming by themselves as stationary objects. But as symbols in a row fading toward the horizon, they vividly suggest the concept of universality—and when the music begins and the toes start tapping, rhythm, too.

Paula Scher's chorus line of shoes is illustrated by David Wilcox.

Political propaganda must not be too obscure, since the goal is to communicate a message immediately and without ambiguity. In the 1968 anti-Vietnam War poster, Tomi Ungerer juxtaposed three elements in a no-frills, surrealistic composition requiring little interpretation. The idea that a Vietnamese is being forced to ingest Miss Liberty (a symbol of American imperialism) is a powerful indictment rendered in Ungerer's satiric line.

Tomi Ungerer's poster is a marriage of three polemical symbols.

Collage is one technical means of achieving interesting juxtapositions, as Altman and Manley's shopping bag to Glendale Galleria, Ivan Chermayeff's poster for "New York and The Arts: A Cultural Affair," and Helene Silverman's cover for *Metropolis* magazine exemplify. But in each, juxtaposition is just one graphic tool among others (including scale change, mixed media, historical referencing, and type play, each of which will be discussed in subsequent sections), bringing the incongruous together as one striking image.

Discordant juxtapositions are key to this bag designed by Brent Croxton and Melina Maniscalo for the Altman and Manley agency.

The more, the merrier, in Ivan Chermayeff's design.

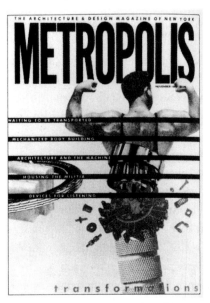

Anomalous relationships add drama to
Helene Silverman's cover.

Repetition

Joseph Goebbels, the infamous Nazi Minister of Propaganda, asserted that if a lie is told enough times, it become true—repetition generates credibility. While only the most simplistic parallel is intended here, many visual artists believe that if something is repeated enough times, it becomes interesting—even funny. Andy Warhol applied this premise to his series of Campbell's Soup Can painting, and took it to a painfully boring extreme with his experimental films in which one scene (the Empire State Building, for example) was repeated and maintained over and over for hours. Like any aspect of art, repetition only works when the idea or object being repeated is inherently interesting or funny; repetition for its own sake, as an end in itself, is a hit-or-miss proposition.

David Wilcox's painting of mating rabbits for Paula Scher's record album design of Eric Gale's *Multiplication* is a clever but obvious play off the title. Dean Hanson's decidedly witty use of repeating "greaser" hairdos in conjunction with the headline "See The Great Oils At The Memphis Brooks Museum" is surprising as a bank advertisement but effective nonetheless. But repetition at its most hilarious is exemplified by the *New York Newsday* cover published on the day after former Philippines First Lady Imelda Marcos was acquitted of fraud and theft charges. Among Mrs. Marcos's alleged crimes, she was accused of buying countless pairs of shoes with squandered taxpayers' money, and throughout her four-week trial, *Newsday* had accompanied its courtroom coverage with daily photographs of her

In Paula Scher's album cover, the title is perfectly underscored by David Wilcox's loving bunnies.

A funny headline and repeating coifs make Dean Hanson's ad sing.

Robert Eisner's Newsday cover is witty and informative.

footwear, captioned as "the shoe of the day." This device, amusing on its own terms, became even better when *Newsday* delivered its punchline, having obviously planned for the day when Mrs. Marcos would *walk* away from court a free woman. (And what did they have planned in the event of her conviction? "Go Directly to Jail"?)

Chuck Carlson relies on scale changes of fun images to achieve surprise.

Scale

Laurel and Hardy and Abbott and Costello are today remembered as much for their emblematic physiques as for a few classic comedy routines. Even if who's who is a blur, the image of fat and thin, short and tall is branded in our memories. These comedians were indeed funny for their slapstick antics, but their humor was definitely enhanced by their looks, with their relative scale changes as the keys. Scale change has a greater effect on our consciousness than any of the other characteristics in this chapter. Remember the film *The Incredible Shrinking Man*? It played off the absurd notion that someone could be reduced to microscopic size in an otherwise normal world, smartly depicting our fears of helplessness and dread of being symbolically small in our own worlds. More recently, *Honey, I Shrunk the Kids* dealt even more farcically with the same subject. Size change has symbolic impact that, as many very short people know all too well, would take a psychologist to explain. So suffice it to say that scale change is also an important design tool, one that if not always funny, certainly contributes to memorability.

Nineteenth-century caricaturists began the convention of using big heads on little bodies as a means of exaggerating facial features and rendering their subjects helpless—like dolls—in their artistic space. Similarly, cartoonists often increase the size of a subject in relation to nature (e.g., a mammoth body menacing the comparatively tiny and hapless planet Earth) as a means of showing empowerment or a great threat. Likewise the design of the 1989 AIGA Minnesota/Design Camp poster, designed by Chuck Carlson, comically uses scale to reinforce the absurdly stylized images. The poster is a two-pronged impression. When folded, the front reveals a shoulder of "camper" appearing on the left-hand side, while above is a silhouette of a humorously decapitated walker throwing off a surreal shadow. When opened to full size, the camper is silhouetted in the foreground with a bunch of nametags stuck to his or her shirt (a witty notion), framed by various smaller objects suggesting the outdoors. The result is not sidesplitting but suggests the good times that Design Camp promises. In a similarly scale-driven poster, Paula Scher's design for Coast to Coast relies on a close crop (also somewhat decapitated) head of a giant woman towering over "tiny" World War II planes flying in formation across her body. The anomalous scale relationship here suggests many absurd possibilities.

Not as menacing, but just as odd, Weiden and Kennedy's ad for Nike's Air Jordan uses scale change to bring home the message that "Michael Jordan has overcome the acceleration of gravity by the application of his muscle power in the vertical plane, thus producing a low altitude earth orbit." Indeed, he is seen flying over a lilliputian Spike Lee and the scientist who presumably made the physics-laden statement, their mouths hung open in disbelief. For added graphic power, they are positioned on top of a miniature photograph of an even more lilliputian planet earth.

HANG TIME

The Cox Group's Dali-esque skyline and Paula Scher's towering woman rely on making the commonplace monumental.

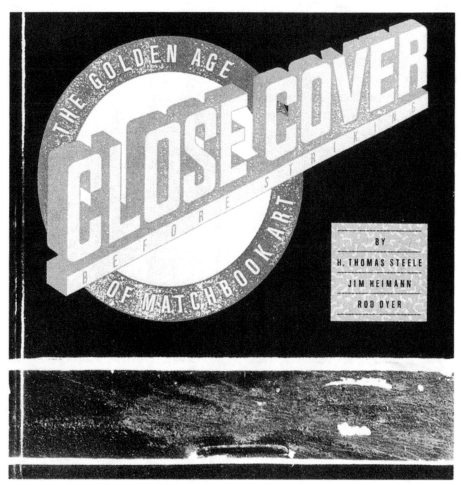

Harriet Baba and Rod Dyer made a matchbook motif gigantic, and it immediately became funny.

Two sunny-side up eggs filling the front and back of a Paula Scher record cover design proves that even a mundane object can be a witty solution when enlarged beyond expected proportions. Similarly, Rod Dyer and Harriet Baba's cover for *Close Cover Before Striking*, a book of matchbook cover art, magnifies the basically tiny matchbook ten times for an impressive display. Playing with two scale changes, Chip Kidd's extreme reduction of a disembodied head precariously floating in space under a portion of a much larger *Q* on the cover of the *Quarterly* 14 makes the letter seem much more menacing than a mere letter should be.

Anthony Russell uses scale as a humorous conceit on the birth announcement for his son, Daniel, which reminds us that for reasons of cuteness and accessibility, we are predisposed to anything lilliputian or miniature—babies, kittens, and so on.

Conveniently, Russell's new baby was exactly the size of a paper merchant's remnant on which the new father printed "Daniel Russell" in foot-wide Pistilli Roman letters, underscored by an arrow spanning the name and a caption, "actual size." To accentuate the joke, a miniature photo of the newborn appears on the bottom of the announcement. A baby is also the focal point for a *Metropolis* cover designed by Helene Silverman, for an issue devoted to designing for children. Here a cute (though disembodied) baby's head is enlarged disproportionately to the other elements of the page. As children themselves have a way of doing, this baby puss serves as a real attention grabber.

Chip Kidd's big Q and little head are cause for a gaffaw.

Common to these pieces is the technique called *silhouetting*. Indeed, for a scale change to be truly shocking or meaningful in two-dimensional space, it is not enough simply to enlarge or reduce a rectangular image, since the mind is prepared to perceive photographs

Anthony Russell's big name and little baby speak volumes.

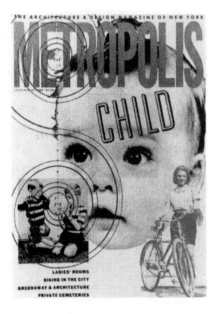

Helene Silverman's big baby draws the eye.

as big or small; to be credible (or *incredible* as the case may be), the scale change must appear extraordinary, an impression best accomplished by isolating the form from its surrounding environment by silhouetting.

But not all scale changes are radical enlargements or reductions. Mike Salisbury's cover for *West* magazine has life-size houseflies crawling over the masthead on an otherwise empty page. In addition to the surprise of seeing these pests on a magazine cover, the intuitive given that the shape of a magazine cover defines its own space makes the flies, though not actually exaggerated one way or the other, appear bigger than life.

Ladislav Sutnar used scale shifts to make this 1931 cover dramatic (and timeless).

Mike Salisbury used actual flies to give his 1969 cover that creepy feeling.

Transformation

The alchemists of old were convinced they could transform lead into gold—a good trick if you can do it—and so were authorized by their noble patrons to spare no expense in the attempt. Given more earthly powers wed to stricter budgetary constraints, today's graphic designers are usually asked to make sow's ears into silk purses. Actually, the alchemists had the easier task—while designers are often called upon to do magic, the reality of how this is achieved is not as simple as having Merlin snap his

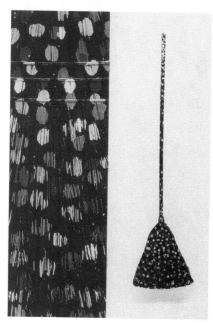

fingers, and *presto*, a frog's a prince!—the process is a little more labor intensive.

We have already discussed distortion, juxtaposition, repetition, and scale change as keys leading to humorous design. But the magic comes when the designer using these tools achieves some kind of transformation by taking the ordinary and making the extraordinary. Actually, like the most effective graphic wit, the best ideas seem effortless—and to a certain extent obvious.

Woody Pirtle transformed the most commonplace household tool, the ordinary broom, into a thing of beauty and wit simply by painting a score of them with odd colors and shapes, photographing them together, and publishing the results as a long, narrow brochure. A poster for Washington Illustration metamorphoses

Woody Pirtle transformed a broom into art. the typical artist's palette into the shape of

Burkey Belser transformed a palette into a map.

Bart Crosby transformed a phone into everyman.

Washington, D.C. Bart Crosby put a shirt, tie, suspenders, and horn-rims on a telephone receiver and *presto*, the perfect cover for the Goldman Sachs Funds Group's *Smart Phone Users Guide*. And Drew Hodges saw that the otherwise blocky MTV logo could be made into a pool table to make a not- so- obvious but original concoction.

The analogy to magic is particularly apt these days. Comic transformation of inanimate objects into human forms and of human forms into inanimate objects can be

The original MTV logo, by Manhattan Design.

attained by a few flips of the computer mouse, the accessibility of which has prompted many designers to play with interesting forms. But this kind of transformation is not necessarily new. One of the earliest "public" uses of photomontage as transformation tool was achieved by John Heartfield with the little mascot for the Dada journal *Jedermann Sein Eigner Fussball* (Everyman His Own Football), in which a

John Heartfield's 1919 collages on the cover of Everyman His Own Football.

Henry Wolf's 1974 cover of Show *transformed the old Bards into new ones.*

Rick Biedel transformed a man into furniture/man.

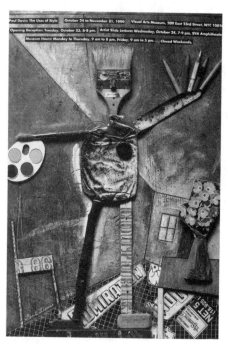

Paul Davis's SVA poster transforms junk into an artifact.

Marc Cohen uses TV dials to make a face.

football man tips his hat to the reader. Decades later, Henry Wolf made a similarly witty manipulation on the cover of *Show* magazine for a story on William Shakespeare. More recently, and without the benefit of the computer, Rick Biedel transformed furniture into "figureheads" in his sprightly campaign for Modernage, a retro furniture store. Employing a three-dimensional collage approach, Paul Davis conjured up the meta-morphic artist from an amalgam of found materials. And using two-dimensional collage, James Hogan illustrated an advertising flyer for San Francisco Focus with a figure made from bridges and assorted cul-tural ephemera.

Jamie Hogan uses bridges as britches.

Among the most common forms of design transformation is making faces from objects. Mark Cohen employed television dials to make a face on the cover of *Inner Tube*, while Sullivan/Perkins blended drawing and televi-sion elements together for a face on the call for entries for the Dallas Society of Visual Communicators. And Linda Shankweiler transformed an abstract design into a head for the musical *Hair*.

Whether used together or separately, these formal design elements can result in amusing images. The next section will show how these tools can contribute more cerebral solutions.

Linda Shankweiler uses cut paper as hair.

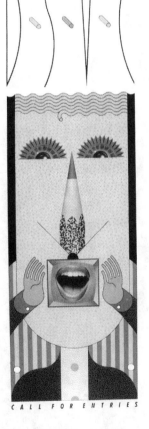

John Flaming uses shapes and objects to make a poster.

The virtue of

Humor

Keeping sane in an inane world.

Peter Girardi

subverts seriousness—the last refuge of the shallow.

 Brian Collins

is surprising, disarming, and human.

 Scott Stowell

Chapter

Puns and the Language of Visual Wit

Visual Puns

Not all graphic wit and design humor falls under the umbrella of the visual pun, but an overwhelming majority of what is good in this book, even though it appears in other chapters for formal or aesthetic reasons, can be called puns, because the visual pun is an image with two or more concurrent meanings that when combined yield a single message. The visual pun forces a viewer to perceive an idea on more than one conceptual level. However, if there is no idea, there is no pun.

Not all puns are humorous in the strictest sense. In *Visual Puns in Design*, Eli Kince states that puns have a "humorous effect" and an "analytical effect." The pun is humorous when a certain cleverness and surprise is created. "That mental jolt creates a humorous 'spark,' which releases tension in the form of a smile or a laugh," he says. The pun is analytical when "symbols used in witty and apt ways are appreciated intellectually more than emotionally." As in language, a pun may be a funny joke, a stimulating intellectual synopsis, or, in certain cases, a real stinker. At the risk of sounding repetitious, puns are best when effortless, not strained. The problem with a bad visual pun is, of course, obvious: While a bad verbal pun dissipates in thin air, its visual counterpart is more permanent. The range of puns here is qualitatively varied, but the real stinkers have been eschewed.

Literal Puns

The literal pun conveys a message without ambiguity. While this implies the absence of humor, such is not the case. These examples show the various media through

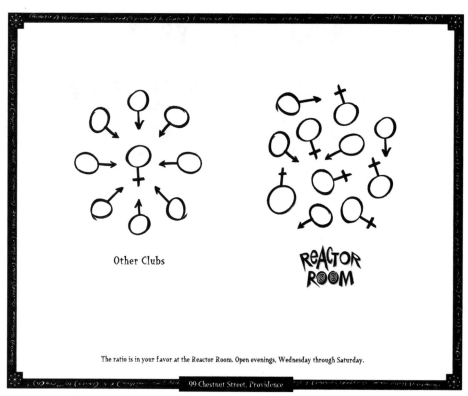

Other Clubs

REACTOR ROOM

The ratio is in your favor at the Reactor Room. Open evenings, Wednesday through Saturday.

99 Chestnut Street, Providence

Symbols for males and females speak volumes in this ad by Rivers, Doyle, Walsh & Co.

Elizabeth Morrow Mackenzie substitutes the word "beauty" for a bodice hugger.

which literal puns are communicated, including object, illustration, photograph, and pictogram. The first example of a three-dimensional object also evidences that some humor is exploitive, if not sexist—this French curve by an anonymous designer is a literal pun because the idea of making a woman into one of these curvilinear drafting templates is a direct substitution of the original meaning. This version shows a curvaceous woman cut from the same fluorescent plastic as real French curves. In Milton Glaser's Olympic poster, he takes apart the Olympic logo and the result is a

A comic "French curve."

ring toss. Glaser throws the rings onto a Greek column, which without an iota of ambiguity conveys the context of Greek games. Willie Baronet's design for a reunion announcement is a three-tiered message: First, the word "reunion" is constructed out of classic yearbook pictures, indicating that this is not just any old congress, but an annual high school event; moreover, this is not just any reunion, either, but the tenth; and coincidentally, the *i* and *o* are easily substituted by the number 10, thus punning on the event and its cycle. Michael McGinn's logo for a department store security agency combines two literal images—a padlock and shopping bag—into one economical mark, while Chiat Day Mojo's NYNEX advertisements use torn-paper puns in the shapes of objects to play off the various Yellow Pages entries. And finally, Seymour Chwast's two posters announcing exhibitions of his work evidence a keen ability to make effortless visual puns. The poster for his Cooper Union retrospective shows his head twisted

Milton Glaser's Olympic ring toss pun.

Willi Baronet's dual use for "10."

Michael McGinn's shopping security logo.

If it's out there, it's in here. **NYNEX** Yellow Pages

Chiat Day built an ad campaign around visual puns.

Seymour Chwast takes the word "retrospective" literally, in a figurative sort of way.

Seymour Chwast blows a visual pun from his worldly pipe.

back (in a play on the word "retrospective," which literally means to look back), looking at a lion through the various symbolic filters an artist uses. In the poster for another exhibition, Chwast's face is completely empty, save for his emblematic pipe, from which a wafting plume of smoke becomes a pun on the map of Brazil, where is show will take place.

Suggestive Puns

The suggestive pun is made by combining two or more unrelated or disparate references, sometimes as a substitution for a more literal reference, conveying two or more meanings.

Woody Pirtle's announcement for a lecture in Iowa combines a drawing of the Chrysler Building as a corncob in a shuck. The suggestion is clear that a city boy has arrived in the country. For UCLA's 1989 Summer Sessions, Pirtle also fabricated a palm tree out of books to suggest not only academics but the tropical southern Californian clime. Douglas Harp combined the acronym AIDS

Woody Pirtle's corny New York.

Woody Pirtle's palm tree.

 **A**I**DS**

Susan and Douglas Harp underscore the urgency of AIDS research.

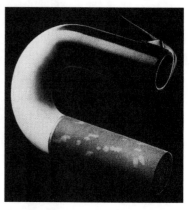

with an hourglass, suggesting that time is running out for victims of this tragic disease. And Rob Boezewinkel suggests that cigarettes are killers in a seamless transformation in which the "cancer stick" turns into a gun.

Rob Boezewinklel's smoking gun.

Verbal/Visual Puns

These are visualizations of aphorisms, sayings, and phrases that are so much a part of our vernacular that the pun is only understandable in that context. For example, "the better mousetrap" is wittily illustrated in Bart Crosby's poster for IDSA's Industrial Design Excellence Awards. "Heat wave" is represented by a melting record in Robert Grossman's illustration of Paula Scher's record of the same title "Making Our Mark" is humorously handled in Chris Hill's splattering of the human hand The O in *SOS*, the international distress warning, is replaced by a globe illustrated by Douglas Harp "Performing live" is illustrated by Woody Pirtle, who sends a Woody Wagon jumping through a hoop (which is also a double entendre on the aphorism "jumping through hoops," suggesting that Pirtle will be forced to do difficult acts of great skill. Finally, Carin Goldberg's cover for the album *Bread Alone* is a pun on the title with a slight twist, for it shows that indeed, man cannot live on bread alone, but needs a touch of champagne to wash it down.

This trademark for an eye doctor is one short of four-eyes.

Robert Grossman's melting vinyl heats up
Paula Scher's design.

Bart Crosby's better mousetrap poster revives
an old saying in a witty manner.

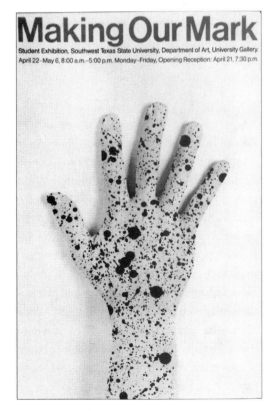

Making Our Mark
Student Exhibition, Southwest Texas State University, Department of Art, University Gallery.
April 22–May 6, 8:00 a.m.–5:00 p.m. Monday–Friday, Opening Reception: April 21, 7:30 p.m.

Chris Hill makes a hand into an action painting.

Woody Pirtle has a "Woody" jumping through hoops.

Susan and Douglas Harp send a strong message on Earth Day.

Carin Goldberg's play with the "Bread Alone" title.

Toys and Playthings

A few years back, a prestigious New York art gallery mounted a Christmas show of artists' toys. In fact, the number of what one might call serious "Sunday toy makers" was impressive, but not really surprising, for artists are inveterate toy makers. For example, few visitors to New York's Whitney Museum of American Art have failed to notice and be smitten by Alexander Calder's circus. His delightful animals, clowns, and circus accoutrements fashioned from pieces of twisted wire and old fabric are a treat for young and old (indeed, perhaps more for the latter, who can thoroughly delight in the artist's unpretentiousness). Calder made his toys as an extension of his creative being. Other artists in the New York gallery show made toys and playthings not for resale but either as respites from their daily routines or as extensions of their canvases or sculptures. In fact, many of these objects are reminders that before the advent of GI Joe, Barbie, and Mutant Ninja Turtles, toys were unpretentious, functional artworks intended to be used, abused, and enjoyed.

Graphic designers and illustrators are no less able, ready, or willing to make toys for limited, personal use. But since commercial graphic artists tend to have a little more business savvy than their fine-arts counterparts, it should not come as a surprise

Byron Glaser and Sandra Higashi make Zolo toys with playful colors and shapes.

that some of these inventions make it into the public arena. Indeed, as the counter-point to mass-produced toys, and consistent with the boutique sensibility of today's retail marketers, certain entrepreneurs are successfully marketing "artist's" toys to the public. Among the most popular, Byron Glaser and Sandra Higashi's Zolo is spiritu-ally influenced by the postmodern penchant for exciting colors and cartoon shapes. Zolo is a collection of amorphic shapes and objects, which, when pieced together (like a superannuated Mr. Potato Head), become uniquely funny figures—part surre-al, part cubist, part fantastic.

Unlike traditionally packaged toys, Zolo comes in boxes that echo the inherent wit of the game inside rather than pandering to the commercial instincts of the seller. In other words, the packaging is every bit as humorous as the toy itself. Likewise, illustra-tor Richard McGuire has transformed his enjoyment making doodles into his Puzzle Head game, a set of interlocking faces that become a composite doodle. He also invent-ed a toy that combines his own comics work with the wonders of modern technology. E-O is a colorful, comic revolving figure that is propelled by a photo-electric cell in its base. While it does not do much more than revolve, and in so doing gives the impres-sion that it is mouthing the vowels "e-o," it is delightfully rendered in orange, blue, and white, and comes in a collectible tube with McGuire's self-designed label. This toy is, however, more than a clever object—it is an extension of the artist's visual storytelling.

Richard McGuire's Puzzlehead is a doodle come to life.

Richard McGuire's EO turns 'round 'n' 'round 'n' 'round.

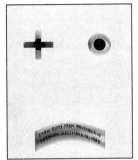

Steven Guarnaccia's invitation to an exhibition is a paper toy.

Steven Guarnaccia is inspired by the old children's face-making toys.

Similarly, some designers use toy-making techniques and special effects to imbue their commercial designs with playful allure, almost like puns of toys. Steven Guarnaccia's die-cut invitation to an exhibition of his work is basically a mini-mask that unfolds to create a three-dimensional sculpture. Guarnaccia (see interview, page 141), bases much of his graphic design and illustrations on the influence of old toys, which he collects almost obsessively. Indeed, the masks shown here, which Guarnaccia designed for the Apple computer company, are derived exclusively from that collection.

Mix-and-match features give this dimension.

Steven Guarnaccia's masks for Apple Computers.

Toy as Pun

The popularity of the Sharper Image store chain in recent years is in direct response to the needs of baby-boomers (the most affluent generation in memory), who grew up with an excess of toys and have the taste for more. This, combined with an increase in electronic gadgetry, has created a new market. These grown-up toy stores are a kind of hybrid of art or museum shops and novelty boutiques, influenced in recent years by a rise in "artists" products and wares in the marketplace. By now, everyone who's anyone owns a Michael Graves teapot, which is really a caricature of a teapot, or a Philippe Starck juicer, which though it looks like a scrunched silver king crab is actually quite functional. Jumping on the bandwagon, certain graphic designers have diversified into the gadget or *tchotchke* market with great zeal and vibrato.

Stephen Doyle's tissue serves dual purposes.

In terms of toylike products, one might have thought T-shirts would become a designer's niche, or that novelties like Stephen Doyle's *Catcher in the Rye* facial tissues might be a close second. Actually, watches are the most common product to emerge from the offices of contemporary graphic designers. Indeed, with the advent of the inexpensive and interchangeable designer Swatch Watch, watches replaced jeans as the preeminent haute design manifestation of the Post-Modernist era. And since a watch is a watch, designers have sought to give meaning to their concoctions by making them into puns. M&Co was the first of many design firms to send their entrepreneurial timepieces into the marketplace. But these are not just conventional wares. M&Co's watches and clocks have numerals in the wrong places, or no numerals at all. The idea was to challenge the senses and bring a smile to the eye as the wearer attempts to decipher the real time.

Comic Swatch Watch by
Steven Guarnaccia

M&Co's jumbled watch face still
keeps good time.

M&Co's reductive watch does the
job, too.

The many faces of Steven Guarnaccia's Box Clox.

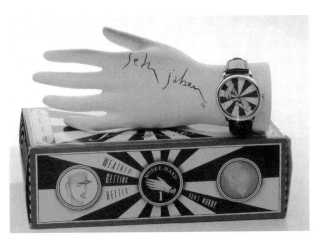

Seth Jaben tells time hypnotically.

As book outlets decrease and the book market becomes more competitive, publishers are testing new gimmicks. One publisher, for example, announced a line of scented books. The obvious ones on gardening and cooking might be cloying but at least make sense; but what about sports books, especially those on wrestling? Ugh. During the Eighties and Nineties Abbeville Press published its "nine by nine" series of books on ephemera and popular Americana, which usually include covers as toys, including some tactile puns: *Bowl O Rama: The Visual Arts of Bowling*, designed by Tommy Steele, had two die-cut holes in the bowling ball appearing on the cover, and the title for *Miniature Golf*, designed by Helene Silverman, was printed on acetate over a patch of "real" Astroturf. In recent years, there have been a surfeit of pop-up, gatefold, even holographic covers and jackets designed to engage the reader's sense of play.

H. Thomas Steele's bowling bowl has three dye-cut holes.

Helene Silverman's cover is made from real Astroturf.

One final note on toys: Arguably, the most satisfying play for a designer is a toy used in real life and indeed is bigger than life (or at least a small toy). For Charles Spencer Anderson, his design for the side of a Litho Inc. delivery truck is the ultimate toy (think Tonka toy truck) come to life. As we've noted in the section on Scale, when type and image are increased to surprising sizes the equilibrium of the viewer is thrown into a tizzy. Such is the impact, and the fun, of Anderson's witty typography on a fast moving vehicle.

Charles Spencer Anderson's real truck is a big toy.

Humor entices a smile, and involves the viewer.

Stefan Sagmeister

Humor is
a chance to elude
the clutches
of the logical mind,
and deliver the
information
to a non-rational
part of the brain.

Josh Gosfield

Whenever you see
females interviewed
on television, they are asked of the
most important
quality in a man.
Usually, they say "sense
of humor."
Then they walk into the sunset
with a rich, boring guy.

Mirko Ilic

Chapter

4

Déjà Vu All Over Again

Nostalgic Wit

Nostalgia. It sounds like an ailment—neuritis, neuralgia, nostalgia. Take a bromo and call me in the morning. In fact, the word was coined in the seventeenth century to describe a severe illness brought about by homesickness afflicting soldiers during the Thirty Years War. In addition to fits of melancholia induced by battle, protracted absences from hearth and home caused these young warriors to experience intense stomach pains and nausea—no laughing matter, to be sure. Yet by the nineteenth century, other terms replaced nostalgia in the medical sense, and the term came to signify a romantic memory of, or dreamlike return to, a more sublime and innocent time and place in history.

We have all been nostalgic for something lost, misplaced, or simply experienced and fondly remembered. But nostalgia is not exclusively a recollection of one's *own* past, but rather of any number of depersonalized an idealized pasts having occurred as far back as eons ago and as recently as yesterday. In art, for example, the late-nineteenth-century pre-Raphaelite Brotherhood of painters, illustrators, and designers who influenced an aspect of turn-of-the-century English decorative art, returned to what they saw as a venerable aesthetic predating the perceived artistic malaise of their own time. They adopted styles and themes that conjured up Merrie Olde England, complete with its Knights of the Round Table, in an attempt to rekindle values long gone but still appreciated. Their vision was intended as a gateway toward new discovery, but rarely resulted in much more than a stylistic conceit—which, incidentally, became a rather comic conceit that might be referred to as the Prince

Valiant approach to art. Indeed, reprising the past for inspiration can be a problem if applied without critical perspective, for the past is not the present, and never will be. Used for its own sake, nostalgia quickly becomes a creative and emotional crutch.

Nonetheless, nostalgia will continue to be popular as long as people choose to experience the past voyeuristically. For this reason, it's also a big business today. Writing about nostalgia as a marketing strategy, Randall Rothenberg reported in the *New York Times* that "the way it was is the way it is." Marketers acutely understand that trading on a legacy, even a fictional or manufactured one, gives consumers of certain products the confidence needed to make their buying choices. The past serves as a pedigree for a company or product, and design is the principal means of communicating this past. However, there was a time when a longing for the *future*—and a rejection of the past—held the same mass appeal as nostalgia does today. The 1939 New York World's Fair was billed "The World of Tomorrow," and predicted the wonders of American civilization twenty years hence. Tomorrowland was once Disneyland's most exciting attraction, offering speculation on commuter space travel and other semifulfilled technological advancements. Throughout America, atomic power was the symbol of progress, and "progress," said General Electric, was their "most important product." In design, everything from logos to exhibitions exalted to *atomania*. This craze for the future was also fueled by the success of manned space travel, which reached its zenith with an American landing on the moon in 1969. Space, "the final frontier," not only gave us *Star Trek* and *The Jetsons*, but also Stanley Kubrick's epic *2001: A Space Odyssey*, which influenced futuristic styles in everything from graphics to clothing to cars. But *2001* was also the beginning of our collective backslide into a nostalgic obsession. Evoking millennia fears, like those experienced at the turn of the nineteenth century, when it was prophesized that industrialization would lead to the end of civilization, *2001* suggested that the future wasn't (or wouldn't be) all it had been cracked up to be: Things could indeed go wrong. Warnings of environmental hazards were routinely ignored and written off as the ravings of crackpots despite the physical evidence that progress was taking its ecological toll. Even a 1964 issue of *Mad* magazine, in one of its more prescient comic features, satirically cautioned about the industrial world's growing waste-disposal problems, suggesting that space shuttles would soon transport refuse into space and leave rings of garbage around the earth and other planets. By the 1970s, fascination with the future began to turn to skepticism. And, finally, with the end of the Vietnam War in 1974, attention turned fully to a new enemy: the byproducts of progress.

Without the prospect of a glorious future to hold the imagination, an idealized past was revived to anchor mass hopes and dreams to something tried and true, with mass media as the conduit and graphic design a principal tool. The first era to be so revived was, ironically, the 1950s, a decade during which Senator Joseph McCarthy had run roughshod over American freedom, rock and roll had been outlawed in schools as aboriginal and animalistic, and African Americans had suffered under Jim

Crow in the American South. But the myth portrayed on television series like *Laverne and Shirley* and *Happy Days*, in movies like *American Graffiti*, and, yes, even in the advertising and graphic design of the period, instead highlighted the fictional heroes of mass media, as well as such pop-cultural ephemera as hoola hoops, Davy Crockett hats, jukeboxes, and '57 Chevys. These and other period symbols were combined into a stylized "retro" graphic vocabulary that was not only unthreatening but also rather silly, especially in light of other, more imaginative contemporary graphic styles.

Many critics have branded the 1950s as an uptight decade, noting its lack of humor. But the nostalgia of the later 1970s and 1980s has had a rehabilitating effect, allowing a generation who never experienced the 1950s to look at the period from a different, more rose-colored vantage point than was available to those who grew up in it. Many 1950s graphic images and letterforms, especially the emblematic scripts, novelty typefaces, trade characters (like Speedy Alka-Seltzer and Reddy Kilowatt) and decorative design ornaments (including liver-shaped lozenges) were reapplied in entirely new contexts. Some designers used these images as codes, serving, for example, as satiric devices counterpointing contemporary fashions. Some designers used the graphic forms for their inherent humor, and still others for the pure aesthetic pleasure of working with appealing graphic forms that would otherwise be considered out of bounds.

Although there is currently a trend toward revived 1960s psychedelia, most subsequent nostalgic direction has been backwards. Graphic ornaments from the 1940s, 1930s, and even the 1920s have become once again ripe for the picking.

Jerry Johnson's 1988 comic homage to 1950s Redi Kilowatt.

Indeed, each of these periods had a more or less identifiable graphic style or code, though one often spilled over into the other (which is understandable—there is no reason to expect graphic trends to respect such calendar-driven notions as decades). During the 1920s, the remnants of Art Nouveau gave way to Art Moderne (or Art Deco) and, more lastingly, the progressively Modern. During the 1930s, Cubistic Art Deco was ubiquitous in Europe, while a variant known as Streamlining developed in the United States. Owing to World War II, the early 1940s were visually austere, yet the late 1940s saw the convergence of many previous stylistic manifestations. Tom Wolfe aptly describes the present confluence of design styles as having derived from a "big closet," which designers turned into a rummage sale, with outmoded style manuals available for pennies and a priceless supply of old forms on hand as well.

It is worth noting that this is not a new phenomenon. The psychedelic poster artists of the late 1960s referred to themselves as "pack rats," borrowing (or in today's art parlance, *appropriating*) past imagery because it either had aesthetic or psychological value or was just simply funny. The new designer pack rats' motives are similar, although their chosen language is quite different from that of their predecessors.

Despite psychedelia's appropriation of East Indian, Native American, Vienna Secessionist, and American Victorian design elements, its graphic language, which also included a rainbow color palette and curvilinear, drug-induced shapes, turned into a distinctly original design language. Indeed, over time, and after intense mainstream co-opting, it became the ambient voice for a youthful, sex, drugs, and rock 'n' roll-inspired constituency. More precisely, psychedelia borrowed from the vernaculars of previous times and places to become the vernacular of its own time and place. We might note here that vernacular is common, everyday language, which is actually how one might define commercial art or graphic design, since their purpose is to communicate to a mass audience in a language that will be understandable to all.

Vernacular Humor

In the 1980s, the word "vernacular" was used rather imprecisely by graphic designers to distinguish naïve, poorly designed, or undersigned printed manifestations from *premeditated* graphic design, or what are now haughtily referred to as graphic communications. This is, of course, is a subjective hierarchical notion based on comparative levels of taste, training, skill, and talent. In fact, work done without an aesthetic sense or design plan, such as a paper coffee cup or a luncheonette menu showing some stock scene of the Parthenon and typeset in some ugly, "default" typeface is not graphic design per se, but common, commercial job printing. Conversely, a paper coffee cup and menu featuring, for example, the OH LA LA logo *is* graphic design, because a graphic designer (not a printer or sign painter) produced it. Vernacular is considered inherently funny not just because most old fashions are considered funny years after the fact but because they represent a time before designers were sophisticated professionals. The vernacular is therefore easy to satirize, because in an era of design sophistication, it is so charmingly naïve.

In the 1960s, American Pop artists began appropriating commercial art, making it monumental and thereby giving it the status of high art. Soup cans, billboards, gas station identity systems, and so on were heralded by art's avant-garde as the "true" American vernacular. Likewise, taking a cue from Robert Venture's *Learning from Las Vegas*, a landmark analysis of indigenous commercial architecture (i.e., kitsch), graphic designers during the 1980s focused on the newly discovered vernacular, either as the brunt of their humor (by exaggerating and distorting these forms) or as a wellspring for new and old processes. In both cases, the unpretentious vernacular was elevated to an *au courant* style, a witty style, because the forms being quoted were so dated that they could not be straight-facedly used without some infusion of irony. Moreover, it was a unique style, because most trained designers would be hesitant to

step into much of the old-fashioned commercial art without imbuing it with a sense of the absurd.

Nostalgic art can be vernacular, but not all vernacular is nostalgic art. In the 1960s, Pop artists were not recalling the past but rehabilitating then-current packaging and signage. Similarly, when New York's M&Co designs a restaurant menu to look like it was slapped together at a print shop instead of being designed at all, it is intended not as a nostalgic evocation of the vernacular but rather as a subtle critique of the opulence and waste inherent in much con-

M&Co's homage to commonplace signs for Restaurant Florent.

temporary graphic design. In fact, M&Co's menus for two New York restaurants, Bellevues and Restaurant Florent, serve two purposes, giving the restaurants warm and witty personalities to contrast starkly with their excessively chic competition, and showing by example that not all graphic design needs costly production tricks to be effective. Therefore, M&Co's appropriation of the vernacular at once codifies a new kind of chic and a certain kind of environmental responsibility. Employing the vernacular has also provided M&Co with a starting point for a distinctive design methodology, involving a breakdown of the popular aesthetics canon with the aim of changing the way clients and customers perceive and respond to printed communications.

Charles Spencer Anderson, on the other hand, emerged as a leading proponent of nostalgic humor during the late 1980s while with the Duffy Design Group of Minneapolis. Armed with a few rare 1930s matchbook advertising manuals, Anderson gave new life to old comic stock vignettes, or what Paul Rand terms "the absolute worst of commercial art. The stuff we [the Modernists] fought so hard to eliminate."

Rand had been practicing for half a century and had lived through many stylistic periods while steadfastly maintaining a distinctive graphic personality based on an aesthetic and intellectual philosophy that transcended fashion. For him, these comic cuts were not vernacular gems but puerile clichés without wit or aesthetic value. He saw no inherent joke in them, nor any justifiable purpose for their being revived except as a refuge for those without original ideas. But Anderson was in his early twenties when he became a practicing graphic designer, and so had limited knowledge of design history, which in turn meant he didn't realize (or at least had no idea *why*) these outmoded forms were considered anathema by the veteran Modernists. His funny bone was quite honestly tickled by them—for Anderson, the cut represented an appealing aspect of popular culture, especially in contrast to graphic design that takes itself too seriously.

For decades, Dover Books has been publishing a variety of stock-cut compendia, from pre-Victorian engravings to 1930s Art Deco vignettes. Some of the same cuts that Anderson exploits have been reproduced previously in Dover's copyright-free volumes, and many designers from various schools of thought have drawn either inspiration or full, unaltered images from these books, thus adding an element of humor to otherwise dry solutions. These period stock cuts can function like seasoning, spicing up a spare or low-budget design, yet, like all seasonings, they should not be applied in excess—for when overused, one is left with a headache.

The Curse of the Cliché

Technically, a cliché is a pattern in clay, which is why clay-based stereotyped printing plates are referred to in the argot of printing as clichés. Of course, a cliché also refers to a saying, idea, or image that is used over and over until it becomes trite. In

Original comic "Howell Cuts," used for all kinds of commercial printing.

Europe, however, the term is used to describe the small, ready-made illustrations sold by printers and typesetters. For our purposes, a visual cliché is something seen so often, and therefore so immediately understandable, that it does not require translation or interpretation. The problem with a cliché, however, is that something so familiar is easy to ignore. Moreover, using clichés usually results in predictable solutions. Yet when compared to verbal platitudes, *visual* clichés are slightly more effective, because familiar visual cues aid in quick comprehension.

When used as a element of an original idea, a cliché can be a mnemonic device that enhances meaning. Take, for instance some very common and universal symbols, like a skull and crossbones, Uncle Sam, and a cornucopia. By themselves, they are recognizable but not inherently interesting or witty. But when placed in absurd or incongruous contexts, these clichés become keys for unlocking less accessible messages. Clichés are thus used best when they transcend their own limited meanings.

Clichés can be transformed into dynamic symbols by scale changes, odd juxtapositions, and radical distortions: A skull and crossbones becomes funnier when a knife and fork replace the bones; Uncle Same appears less conventional when his stovepipe hat turns into lettering; and a cornucopia—well, actually, it's quite difficult to transform a cornucopia into anything *but* a cliché! In addition, clichés can be made fresh simply by the physical nature of a design and its context. And even the old cornucopia can appear somewhat original given the right application of color or type.

The surrealist painter Max Ernst used trite nineteenth-century magazine engravings as the basis for his wordless collage "novels," such as his masterpiece of absurdity, *La Semaine De Bonte*. By cutting and seamlessly pasting animal head, flowers, and body parts onto other disparate images, he made new visual discoveries. Doing so, he transformed a collection of visual clichés into exciting representations with new meanings. Historically speaking, collage is one of the primary media through which many other artists have transformed visual clichés into uniquely imaginative, often humorous conceptions. Indeed, German Dadaists Raul Hausmann, Hannah Hoch, and George Grosz all borrowed their graphic props from a wide variety of commercial printer's manuals, which were then constructed into seemingly random compositions that were really sophisticated, premeditated political and social commentaries. John Heartfield, another leading Dadaist, combined original photographs and stock (or clichéd) photographs into montages, resulting in some of the most acerbic and memorable political propaganda of the 1930s.

Someone once wrote that the truths of today are the clichés of tomorrow. Indeed, given the spate of design annuals on the market, many truly original ideas quickly devolve into clichés because of designers' habits of following stylistic and conceptual trends. During the 1980s, some very unique design conceits became clichés, possibly because they were too inextricably wed to style in the first place, or because abusive stylists copied and misused them. What began as a collection of humorous, Post-Modern ornaments, such as blips, leader dots, sawtooth rules, and arrows, became stock visual cues for hip design. By the end of the decade, they were so overused that they became soporific, at which point they were ultimately rejected.

The Humorous Icon

Like clichés, icons are familiar, yet not all icons are clichés. Icons are symbols that somehow never lose their currency. That's why all humor, especially political and social humor, features the desecration of icons as a recurring device. Few things are more outrageous than a caustic comedian's impersonation of a famous (or infamous) politician or world leader. Indeed, when caricaturists unmask a public figure through visual exaggeration, they've exposed folly more efficiently than virtually any investigative news story about malfeasance.

The Old Testament tacitly gives its approval to this kind of caricature when Moses urges obliteration of false icons. Yet icon desecration in Christianity is technically a sacrilegious act because icons were originally sacred images—"artistic" representations of Christ. Today, icons are much less sanctified, for twentieth-century Western society has *canonized*, somewhat indiscriminately, many persons high and low. Among the worthy, Wolfgang Amadeus Mozart, Johann Sebastian Bach, Vincent van Gogh, and Winston Churchill are all icons. But because today's icons are not beyond reproach, characters like Adolf Hitler, Richard Nixon, and Ronald Reagan are icons as well. These latter figures have become iconic for their "accomplishments," and hence have been imbued with symbolic attributes. Good or bad, each has become a paradigm or sorts: Bach for his genius, Hitler for his evil, and Reagan for his senility.

Iconic paintings and sculpture, like iconic personalities, are often used to humorous advantage, and certain historical styles also possess symbolic powers. When Seymour Chwast created three hundred "portraits" of Bach to commemorate the composer's three-hundredth birthday

The National Lampoon *send-up of an earless Van Gogh.*

For Bach's three hundredth birthday Seymour Chwast rendered three hundred pictures of the maestro,
each in graphic styles pegged to each year.

in the book *Happy Birthday Bach*, the idea was to represent Bach during every year since his birth, including those long past his death. Bach was caricatured in the context of each particular year, usually in a style appropriately representative of the given period. In so doing, Chwast not only affectionately satirized Bach the icon, but also employed iconographic styles as recognizable signposts. Chwast used accessible historical references as comic backgrounds, adding another level of irony to the portrait.

The American flag flies high on the list of the world's most powerful symbols. Like all flags, it is a mnemonic device, but its simple design evokes complex, often contradictory responses—while it symbolizes freedom, liberty, and bounty, it simultaneously suggests military and economic power used for good and evil. As the ultimate symbol of America, it must remain various things to various people. Kit Hinrichs celebrated the flag in his book, *Stars & Stripes* (Chronicle, 1988), allowing ninety-six designers and illustrators the freedom to "redesign" Old Glory based on their own political or aesthetic motivations in any way they saw fit.

Predictably, many of the images are sardonic commentaries, while others are simply formal exercises; some are witty, others serious. Indeed, Chris Hill's design for the cover is a clever visual pun: The flag is composed of red, white, and blue pencil points, referring, of course, to the artists' interpretations inside.

Institutional icons are also tools (and targets) of the visual humorist. The institution of marriage, for instance, is often addressed, and while it may be stretching the term, there can be no institution more *human* (or indeed more iconic) than motherhood. As you'll recall from earlier in this volume, Herb Lubalin's most memorable and endearing visual pun is the 1967 typographic treatment for the *Mother & Child*

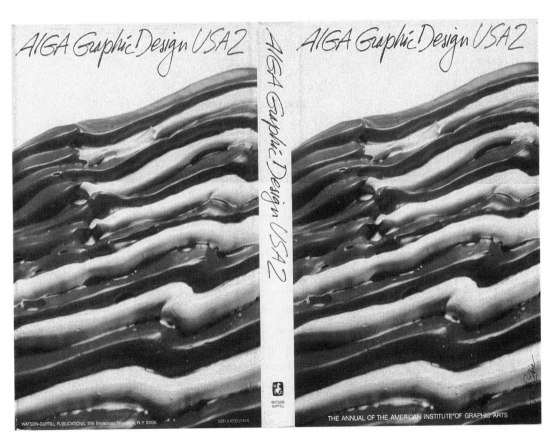

Saul Bass turns paint swirls into Old Glory.

logo, in which the ampersand and the word *Child* fit comfortably inside the *o* of *Mother*, with *Child* nestled in an identifiably fetal position. Turning to a more illustrative approach, the 1976 issue, number 64, of the *Pushpin Graphic*, devoted to "Mothers," carried illustrations of the mothers of such famous artists as Giotto, Toulouse-Lautrec, Juan Gris, and Jackson Pollack, each skillfully rendered by Pushpin's illustrators in the manner of the sons' respective "mature" styles.

Icons can be made humorous in a variety of ways. Exaggeration and distortion, as in caricature, are the most common. But caricature is not just limited to public faces—Seymour Chwast's covers for *Design & Style*, for instance, are actually caricatures of historical art icons, in which he twists, distorts, and reinterprets the essence of old styles and places them in a contemporary context.

The Joy of Parody

Art is a process of making icons, sometimes even unintentionally, for freezing time, space, and even emotion into permanent form. Parody, meanwhile, is the "art" of imitating a serious subject in a nonsensical or ridiculous manner (but generally with underlying intent). The most striking art icons include da Vinci's *Mona Lisa*, Michelangelo's *David*, Picasso's *Les Demoiselles d'Avigon*, Magritte's *Ce n'est pas un Pipe*, and, of course, Grant Wood's *American Gothic*. With the exception of *American Gothic*, which has earned more praise than it really deserves, these are undeniably great works of art that aesthetically transcend their respective places in time, and it should come as no surprise that some of the most recurring visual parodies are made of these works. Parody has made *American Gothic* such a charged symbol that *Life* magazine devoted a feature story to its various incarnations. Magritte's parodists (and copyists) are so numerous in editorial, advertising, and graphic design that a book-length examination of the phenomenon was published in France, with the ironic title *Ce n'est pas un Magritte*. Parodies of classic artworks range from witty reinvention to silly cliché, yet all are essentially visual puns, since they play on two or more applications of one image.

In recent years, historicism has influenced the work of contemporary graphic designers, leading to the development of a number of exclusively graphic design

Seymour Chwast makes a Mondrian painting into floor tiles—and why not?

ILLUSTRATORS SOUTH 85

MEMPHIS ACADEMY OF ARTS, FEBRUARY 28 THROUGH MARCH 29

OPENING RECEPTION, FEBRUARY 28, 5:30 P.M.-8:30 P.M. EXHIBITION OPEN MONDAY THROUGH FRIDAY, 8:30 A.M.-4:30 P.M. SATURDAY 10 A.M.-12 NOON

24
Crayola®
CRAYONS
Different
Brilliant Colors

POSTER: Design: Eddie Tucker
Illustration: Danny Smythe
Typesetting: Lettergraphics
Photography: Allen Mims
Separations: Memphis Engraving Co.
Paper: Western Paper Co.
Printing: B&M Printing

Danny Smythe's illustration owes a debt to René Magritte.

icons. Designs in the form of posters by the Russian Constructivists El Lissitzky and Alexander Rodchenko, the French posterist A. M. Cassandre, and the Swiss photomontagist Herbert Matter have either been quoted, parodied, or otherwise osmosed into the working language of Post-Modernism. While parody does serve an educative function, historical references presented to designers unaware of the original's design contexts can also become an exclusive in-joke, especially if the references are too elitist or obscure.

Despite its recurrence as a method of graphic wit and design humor, parody is one of the most difficult methods to achieve successfully. If the parodist takes too many liberties, then the parody will suffer; conversely, if the material is not twisted enough, the result could read as mimicry, or, worse, plagiarism. If the object of the parody is not universally known—or is known only by a few members of the targeted audience—then, at best, the result might be an interesting design but not a successful parody. For example, Seymour Chwast proposed a poster to Pizza Hut, based on El Lissitzky's supposedly well-known "Beat the Whites with the Red Wedge" poster, showing a triangular wedge carved out of a circle. As parody, it was also a witty pun, since the abstract geometry of Lissitzky's composition could indeed been seen as a slice of the pie. Unaware of the historical references, however, the client saw only an unacceptable design solution. Using the same reference, Pentagram/New York designed a brochure cover for Elektra Records in which Lissitzky's white circle was replaced by an LP record. Whether the client or the brochure's recipients understood the reference is unknown, but the piece was indeed published. Paula Scher's poster for Swatch Watches is a clever parody of one of Herbert Matter's most impressive late-1930s Swiss Tourist Board posters. Matter's photomontages were ubiquitous in Switzerland and are reproduced often in poster collections, but few recipients of the message would have understood the reference when Scher conceived her parody.

Variations of an original (left) El Lissitzky poster by Harold Burch/Pentagram (middle) and Seymour Chwast (right).

Herbert Matter's Swiss tourist poster (left) parodied by Paula Scher.

Was it, therefore, unsuccessful? As a parody, yes, but it had the curious effect of introducing a generation of designers to the legacy of Matter, and perhaps even to Swiss design.

One of the most effective parodies of graphic design is Woody Pirtle's twist on Milton Glaser's Dylan poster, in which Bob Dylan's silhouetted profile is replaced by Glaser's distinctive visage. In place of the huge shock of rainbow-patterned hair that so brilliantly characterized Dylan, Glaser's pate was emphasized by a receding rainbowed hairline. (Incidentally, Glaser's original design was based on a rare silhouetted self-profile drawn decades before by Marcel Duchamp—an homage of which most viewers are unaware.)

The most common design parodies, however, are not parodies of design icons but of books and magazines, requiring a graphic designer to adhere religiously to an original format. Even a simple typeface alteration or a slight deviation from standard folio treatment can break the spell of this sort of parody. During the 1978 New York City newspaper strike, which completely shut down the three major dailies, a *New York Times* mysteriously appeared on the newsstands. In fact, it was *Not The New York Times*, a parody so visually precise that it forced a double take. Of course, since New Yorkers were starved for news during the three-month strike, *Not The New York Times* was a hit, and not only for its brilliant parody of the *Times*—for those readers deprived of their daily newsprint "fix," it was a like a synthetic substitute. A few years later, a parody of the *New York Times Book Review* failed to cap-

Milton Glaser's Dylan poster (left) parodied by Woody Pirtle.

ture the visual and textual essence of the publication, reminding us that successful parody is never easy.

Not The New York Times was a direct parody of a major institution in the tradition of the *Harvard Lampoon* and later *National Lampoon*, but sometimes parodists, like body snatchers, will use the formats of well-known publications for *indirect* parody. Such was the case with *Dogue*, a 1987 send-up of *Vogue*, wherein chic canines were substituted for haute-coutured women. With this type of parody, fidelity to the original design format is ostensibly irrelevant, since the host publication merely serves as a convenient vehicle.

These parodies were initiated by outsiders; when parody is done by insiders, it is called *self-parody*, and is sometimes more difficult to achieve, due to an overfamiliarity with the material. In 1983, *Print* magazine asked Paula Scher and me to write and design a parody issue of their publication. While the format was easy to parody, the content was difficult. Was the parody to be of the magazine itself (a confluence of diverse though related articles about design), without a common stylistic thread? Or was graphic design itself a better target for satire? The latter course, which was eventually chosen, offered many possibilities, including preposterous articles on how Walter Keane, the once-fashionable painter of big-eyed children, influenced American illustration; a fictional interview with Anale Retentiv, an orthodox Swiss designer; Renoir's lost commercial art; the corporate identity of Canada; and a profile of the design of Lubevitch & Moscowitz, famed "deli designers." It can be argued

M&Co's advertisement for Restaurant Florent sends up an old agricultural chart.

that this last article, playing off common deli and luncheonette waiter's checks, sign-boards, and menus, was not so preposterous as it initially seemed, and is, in fact, the basis for much of what we refer to as vernacular design, directly related to some of M&Co's work for Restaurant Florent. In fact, an article satirizing regional design for this parody issue further emphasized this point by awarding first place in a design competition to a common traffic sign. Scher's *Print* cover may also have been influential on the current trend in absurd information design—her illustration, a send-up of a family tree, predates similar applications in *Spy* magazine.

Familiarity Breeds and Breeds

Mark Twain said, "Familiarity breeds contempt—and children," which may be only partly true about human relations but is all too true when referring to graphic design and illustration. Moreover, graphic wit and design humor suffer most from overuse. Shakespeare, presaging the problems caused by design competitions that publicize the best of the new and thereby give common currency to uncommon ideas, wrote, "Sweets grown common lose their dear delight." Though design humor must touch the chord of recognition to be effective, it still must be surprising. Familiar cues are necessary, but an overdose of any one conceit, trick, or otherwise wonderful idea can kill wit. And so, to draw upon a variation of that familiar bromide one last time, "Though familiarity may not breed contempt, it takes the edge of admiration."

IT'S REVENGE.
IT'S LIFE AGAINST DEATH.
IT'S REJUVENATING.
HUMOR
DISTRACTS THE DOMINANT HALF OF THE BRAIN (BUREAUCRATIC) SO THAT THE
OTHER HALF
(LUDIC, POETIC, ONEIRIC) IS ENGAGED. SUDDENLY
WE THINK IN STEREO.

Peter Blegvad

The virtue of wit... pleasure

Jeffrey Keyton

Chapter

Typeplay

Distempered Alphabets

The most witty *and* acerbic typefaces perhaps in the entire history of type were designed during the 1990s. While the late nineteenth century was known for its flamboyant novelty faces, and the Twenties saw a typographic revolution in the form of ascetic geometric types, the Nineties were, for better or worse, the era of functionally dysfunctional yet often riotous faces. The Macintosh not only brought the arcane craft of type design (or fontography) to the masses, which it did by making fonts accessible to everyone through the ease of a keystroke, but also enabled graphic designers who ordinarily used existing typefaces to design their own type families, including a wide array of distressed, distorted, and distempered variations. These typefaces helped define their graphic era and served to excite the printed matter that exemplified the postmodern age.

Digital technology changed the relationship that designers, illustrators, and other artists had to letterforms. Since the turn of the century, artists had included letterforms in paintings and drawings, and some even designed alphabets for artistic and poetic works, but on the whole creating commercial fonts was an uncommon practice. Type manufacture was too work intensive and craft driven. During the 1930s and 1940s modish designers drew stylish alphabets for their own use and amusement, but only a few of these were actually transformed into fonts for widespread distribution. Later, in the Sixties, some designers created one-off faces for companies like Photolettering Inc., and Milton Glaser and Seymour Chwast, among them, designed a few comic alphabets that were in sync with their own eclectic page and poster

ABCDEFGHI

ABCDEFGHI

Milton Glaser's Baby Teeth outline and bold alphabets.

Seymour Chwast's Beastial Bold alphabet.

Ed Fella's quirky Outwest typeface.

designs. Glaser's blocky stair-step face, appropriately named Baby Teeth, and Chwast's cartoon Bestial Bold were lampoons of conventional types that may have been produced commercially, but were exceptions to the rule that typefaces for everyday use were created by skilled craftspeople and artisans trained in the nuances of letterform design. By the late Eighties the personal computer changed that rule (somewhat).

Graphic designers, who before the Macintosh came into the design world would not have designed alphabets because of the time and expense involved, became prodigious creators. The new technology demanded the overhaul of old faces for digital applications and, in addition, allowed for experiments that challenged commonly held standards of legibility, readability, and accountability. At the same moment in history, the tight Modernist control of design and the strict grids that many designers had used were loosening up. Rather than embrace rational functionalism, or any of the older generation's ways, young designers were interested in expressive eclecticism, and this was in large part manifest in the quirky typefaces that were earning popularity through frequent use in youth culture magazines, such as *Beach Culture* and *Ray Gun*. To meet an increased demand for novel and novelty faces a slew of digital type foundries were founded, the pioneer of which was Emigre Graphics, the publisher of *Emigre* magazine (the clarion of digital typography). In addition to launching a creative digital type revolution, Emigre inspired both type and graphic designers to create witty typefaces that were sometimes derived from (and often satirically commented on) classic faces, or were unique, original oddities influenced by things other than typefaces. One such was Outwest, designed by Ed Fella, composed of intersecting oval outlined shapes curiously resembling cowboy hats and cactus. It was at once abstract and representational, stylistic and utilitarian, progressive yet acceptable. It also typified a sense of ironic humor inherent in the new typography. Fella's typeface, like many of the others produced in great numbers from the late Eighties through the Nineties, might be viewed as a simple joke, but it also functioned like any effective display face—to help express messages and ideas. For Fella type, was a new (old) medium that allowed self-expression, but for designers who used the face in their layouts it was a way to design work that looked as though it was in tune with the zeitgeist. The inherent humor of the face was certainly a formidable communication tool.

This new wave of quirky type was, however, more than a vessel for words and ideas; it was a code for a young generation—occasionally a signpost of rebellion, but more often a banner of style. Distressed and goofy type helped convey genuinely new ideas, but it was also a marketing hook for consumables that appealed to youth. Such is, of course, the nature of anything branded au courant.

In addition to Emigre, digital type foundries including House Industries, Garage Fonts (the name signaled the grunge spirit of the faces produced there), The Apollo Program, Thirst, Plazm, and T-26 released a continuous array of types that defied

Letterforms by Gary Panter drawn in pen and ink.

convention. Their daft designs were obvious enticements, but another component of allure was the oddball names the designers gave the faces. For example, Six Gun Shootout & Telegraphic Junction, designed by Marcus Burlile and distributed by T-26 is a raunchy gothic face made even more amusing by the silly name. T-26's The Insanity Set, a family of ten grungy fonts, including Burnout, Droplet Regular, and

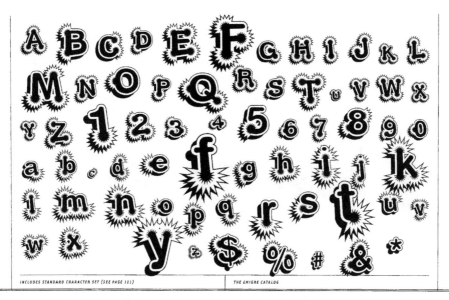

Jigsaw Drop Shadow typeface by Elliott Earls, distributed by Emigre Fonts.

Six Gun Shootout (left) and Telegraph Junction (right) are typefaces by Marcus Burlile, distributed by T-26.

Entropy, by various designers, evoked a sense of play through both names and forms. And Fung Foo & Fufanu, designed by Lee Basford and James Glover for T-26, is a comic-looking, Japanese-character-inspired set of letters that suggest *Blade Runner*–like futurism and is guaranteed to add an ironic charm to any layout. From the turn of the century, type names have been used to add dimension to, describe the

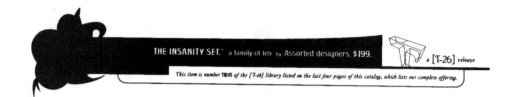

THE INSANITY SET.™ a family of ten by Assorted designers. $199.

a [T-26] release

This item is number T810 of the [T-26] library listed on the last four pages of this catalog, which lists our complete offering.

These fonts are included in The Insanity Set™ I. They are listed in the order shown, from top to bottom.
Commonworld,™ Burnout,™ Morire Open,™ Finial Regular,™ Osprey,™ Neo,™ Entropy,™ Droplet Regular,™ Mattress,™ Tetsuo Organic,™ Moore895 Regular,™ Sidewalker Regular.™

T-26's The Insanity Set, a collection of functionally dysfunctional alphabets.

FUNG FOO™ & FUFANU™ a set of four styles. by Lee Basford & James Glover (FLUID). $59. a [T-26] release

This font is number 10237 of the [T-26] library listed on the last five pages of this catalog, which lists our complete offering.

ABCDEF
OPQRST

abcdefghijklmnopqrstuvwxyz

abcdefgh
ijklmnopqr
stuvwxyz

({{[1234567890]}})

abcdefgh
ijklmnopqr
stuvwxyz

({{[1234567890]}})

from top to bottom: Fufanu,™ regular & italic.

Lee Basford and James Clover's Fung Foo & Fufanu futuristic fonts, distributed by T-26.

essence of, or memorialize the creator associated with a face or family, but in the Nineties names were even more essential in establishing an ironic aura or gestalt. In fact, the names were not unlike rock bands.

In addition to the faces themselves, typographic jewelry—known as fleurons or dingbats—has long been an ancillary component of many alphabet families. These include borders, rules, icons, and other graphic notations. Nineties typographic humor was often best expressed through these pictorial and decorative accou-

Examples of Ed Fella's Fella Parts, distributed by Emigre Fonts.

trements. Ed Fella's Fella Parts and Bob Aufuldish's Zietguys for Emigre were assorted sketches, doodles, emblems, and symbols that were used to inject comedy into typographic treatments and levity into graphic compositions—sometimes they served as rebus-like elements in place of letterforms. This was certainly the case with Marcus Burlile's Spare Parts and Chip Wass's Chippies by Wassco, both for T-26, which are actually small cartoon elements and vignettes that could be used large as

Examples of Marcus Burlile's Spare Parts, distributed by T-26.

comic illustrations or tiny as mini-dingbats. The new digital media was perfect for doodlers to create countless sets of outlandish iconography, but sometimes the doodles went beyond the obviously functional into the land of absurdity. Peter Girardi and Chris Capuozzo's Funny Garbage 1, designed for T-26, is a selection of variegated patterns, drawings, and printer's errors—total junk, really—that might be used to

Chip Wass's iconographic "Chippies by Wassco" distributed by T-26.

make a layout more anarchic. Similarly, Jim Marcus's Fluxus 6 is a collection of geometric shapes and other graphic detritus that look as though they've been Xeroxed dozens of times. They have an inherently comical aura, and the concept behind them is to include on layouts as meaningless decorative material.

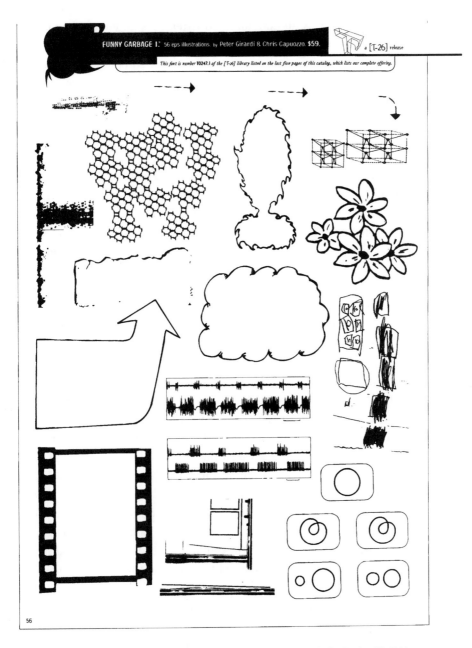

Peter Girardi and Chris Capuozzo's *Funny Garbage 1*, a set of graphic detritions and doodles distributed by T-26.

As this typeplay became increasingly more popular, it also lost some of its appeal. This reaction to stylistic overload next gave way to a light-hearted form of raw hand-lettering, a sometimes humorous style that prevails today. Brush and pen lettering was, of course, common earlier in the century with a comic strip-inspired typefaces like Howard Trafton's Cartoon. But today hand-scrawls are even more commonplace, because with the right computer program, any such notation can be transformed into a digital alphabet with ease. While not all hand lettering is inherently humorous, a wide range of comic- strip–inspired lettering and other so-called hand drawn ver-nacular letterforms have an inherent in sense of humor when practiced by the right hands, of course. And as the computer offers greater perfection, designers are drawn to the imperfection—and wit—that the hand can offer.

Jumbled Letters

The ransom-note school of graphic design dates back to the nineteenth century, when job printers carelessly mixed disparate styles of wood type together on the same poster or bill, resulting in an anarchic visual effect. This emblematic Victorian typog-raphy was born as much of necessity (printers did not always have complete fonts on hand, and so were forced to use what was available) as of an intent to purposefully achieve visual exuberance. Since urban streets and boulevards were becoming increasingly cluttered with posters and advertisements in the late 1800s, it should come as no surprise that printers went through typographic contortions to attain novel, witty, and eye-catching prominence. While elegance is its own reward, rau-cousness (even anarchy) has certain virtues, too, particularly when the purpose is to capture and hold a reader, viewer, or customer. In any design period, designers with high levels of aesthetic consciousness will always strive for balance, harmony, and, of course, legibility, yet just as often there will be renegades to enliven (or degrade) the printed page, often by breaking typographic rules. Though not the first and certain-ly not the last, the Italian Futurists and German Dadaists targeted the nineteenth century's canon of legibility as a symbol of old-fogyism. Vanguard Futurist and Dadaist typographic designers violently dismantled theretofore accepted standards by producing hysterical type that was not simply a metaphor for the new order but the archetype of a distinctly new visual language.

The jumbled letter compositions shown in this section descend from various art-historical sources, including Victorian, Dada, and Surrealism. They are inspired by comics and comic books, bad job printing, and, of course, those clichéd ransom notes that Ray Elliot of Bob and Ray referred to in one of their classic comic rou-tines as having too many *san sareefs*. Funny letters can be handmade (drawn or drafted) somewhat randomly, without regard for uniformity, or they can be bas-tardized versions of real type, essentially cut and pasted for heightened comic results. But whatever the medium, the intent is to throw the eye off balance, and so, too, the equilibrium.

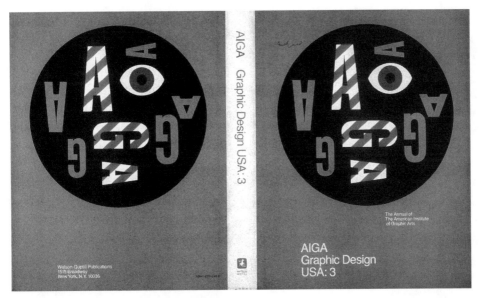

Paul Rand wanted readers to decipher the jumbled letters and images.

Rand's carnival-like composition, made from vintage letters and ornament.

Rand's running man is made from disparate letters and torn papers.

Funny Faces

Goudy Stout is not a syrupy malt beverage but a rare, quirky typeface designed in 1930 by America's leading type designer, Frederic W. Goudy. One step above comic book lettering, it has only one truly positive attribute: It's A seems to be based on the comic gait of Charlie Chaplin's famed Little Tramp. "In a moment of typographic weakness," Goudy later wrote, "I attempted to produce a 'black' letter that would interest those advertisers who like the bizarre in their print." Although he might protest otherwise, the requisites of the advertising business were clear when he made this minor folly; attention in the growing marketplace was not going to be wrested by elegant or classic typefaces, but by eye-catching combinations of letterform and image. The odder the letter, the better. Funny or novelty letterforms and typefaces, many from bygone eras, were therefore called to action in the competitive war to win consumer attention. In fact, many respected type designers added their own weird types to a growing library of faces used for everything from leaflets to billboards.

ABCDEFG
HIJKLM
NOPQRST
UVWXYZ
G & . , -

Goudy Stout is Frederic Goudy's wittiest typeface—especially the A, with its comic gait.

111

One should not, however, ascribe this to the "when bad type happens to good designers" syndrome. Some of these novelty faces are actually quite beautiful (e.g., A. M. Cassandre's Bifur and Morris Fuller Benton's Broadway, and many more are truly humorous, or are at least used in humorous contexts. Novelty typefaces have an interesting history dating back to the early nineteenth century, owing to the industrial revolution and the subsequent development of commerce. In *Printing Types: An Introduction* (Beacon Press, 1971), Alexander Lawson writes that the new typographic fashion began in the early 1800s, when English typefounders produced "a variety of embellished types designed to emphasize their unique characteristics for the single purpose of attracting attention. Fat aces, grotesques, and Egyptians—decorative types when compared to the romans, which had undergone minor changes since the Italian fifteenth century—were not flamboyant enough for the new requirements of advertising display." This sparked furious competition among typefounders to outdo each other in the production of ornamented and fancy faces. One of the most well-known fancy faces, called Rustic in England or Log Cabin in the United States, was designed at the Vincent Figgins Foundry in 1845 and is still in currency today, albeit certainly not for body text and only for limited appropriate uses (like public signage).

The fashion for ornamented, fancy, and novelty faces comes and goes. Recently, however, some vintage specimens have been revived to give an explicitly humorous edge to contemporary visual communications. Semiotically speaking, Log Cabin is perfect for imparting the idea of the great outdoors. Lariat, and its variant, Roy Rogers Bold, unambiguously signal a Western theme. A revived 1930s trifle called Vulcan suggests the motion and speed of that streamlined era, while Howard Trafton's Cartoon, a brush letter that looks as it sounds, and Ice House, a face with a frozen top, are ubiquitous in 1950s retro design. And Milton Glaser's Baby Teeth, shown earlier, derived from popular Italian Art Deco alphabet, while it may not look like any human bicuspids, is a spirited design signaling a basic lightheartedness.

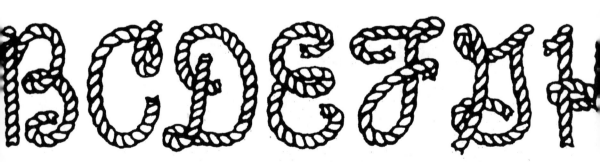

The typeface "Lariat" is perfect for weddings and bar mitvahs with western themes.

"BOLD DISPLAY"

ABCDE
FGHIJK
LMNOP
QRSTU
VW&YX

"Modern Alphabets on Parade"

abcdef z hgijkl
mnopqrstuvwxy

Bold Display is one of many novelty typefaces of the 1930s.

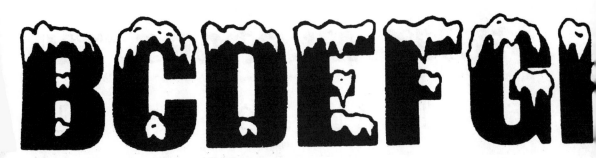

The typeface Frost is perfect either for ice cream trucks or bar mitvah's with artic themes.

113

FGHIJKLMNOPQRSTUV

SAGUARO—CREATED IN THE SPIRIT OF THE GREAT SONORAN DESERT—24PT. TO 96PT.

FGHIJKLMNOPQRSTUV

CURLY-Q—A NEW TWIST ON A PREVIOUSLY RELEASED FAMILY—48PT. ONLY

FGHIJKLMNOPQRSTU

TREEHOUSE (ADAPTED FROM SAWYER EXTENDED)—A REAL TREASURE—24PT. TO 144PT. (SPECIFY GRAIN DIRECTION)

FGHIJKLMNOPQRSTU

SCHOOL BLOCK LEFT—A GRADUATE OF SCHOOL BLOCK RIGHT—36PT. TO 108PT. (BLOCK HEIGHT)

FGHIJKLMNOPQRSTU

BEDROCK OUTLINE—1001 USES—60PT. AND 72PT. ONLY

DEFGHIJKLMNOPQRSTUVW

MUNSTER SOLID—BLOODY GOOD, WHATEVER YOUR TYPE—24PT., 48PT. AND 60PT. ONLY

CDEFGHIJKLMNOPQRSTUVWX

LEGIBILITY MAY BE A PROBLEM, BUT TRUE-BLOODED AMERICANS WILL KNOW WHAT THE MESSAGE IS WITHOUT HAVING TO READ IT

EFGHIJKLMMNOPQRSTUVW

CHOP-STIX—A FORTUNE OF ORIENTAL FLAVOR—24PT. TO 96PT.

FGHIJKLMNOPQRSTU

BANG-BANG—GUARANTEED TO ADD SPARK TO ANY JOB—12PT. TO 60PT. (NOT RECOMMENDED BELOW 24PT.)

FGHIJKLMNOPQRSTU

FRENCH FRY—A CRISP ADDITION—48PT. ONLY

For the typographer who has everything, here is a selection by Richardson and Richardson of typical novelty faces—from Chop-stix to French Fry.

114

The number of funny faces far exceed the capacity of this book if one includes the multitude of expressive novelty faces that were stylized period types and have, with time, become inherently humorous due to changes in fashion. (For a comprehensive showing, Dover Books offers a vast array, as do the various out-of-print type-specimen books available at flea markets and second-hand book emporia.) Shown here is but a small sampling of the short-lived, long-lasting, and current attempts as achieving typographic comedy.

Metamorphic Lettering

If the Trajan inscription is the paradigm of roman letterforms, then the Gellone Sacramentarium, dating from between 755 and 787 A.D., is perhaps the archetype of metamorphic, even comic, lettering. This ancient document is one of the finest examples of how illuminators transformed figures of man and beast into individual letters, a practice that ultimately led to the development of printing and beyond. In ancient times, metamorphic letters also served as sacred metaphors and allegories, communicating either complex tales or simple messages. Playing off the relationship of, say, an object to a letterform, typographic metamorphosis can also be a form of visual punning.

Rap Typography

Milton Glaser once said, "Young artists must make their own discoveries, even if they are old discoveries"; the Bible says there is nothing new under the sun. Therefore, designers currently engaged in the practice of distorting, contorting, and otherwise extorting type to approximate sound or sound bites are not doing anything that hasn't already been done by their elders or betters. Type learned to speak centuries ago, and was given dialects the instant more than one variation of the Roman alphabet was developed. Each type family includes a unique voice, with the variations within that family functioning like regional accents. As the primary means of communication for centuries, type has extraordinary powers that are often taken for granted.

"Words," wrote the British novelist Somerset Maugham, "have weight, sound and appearance. Words make sentences. And type makes those sentences good to look at and good to listen to." Lewis Carroll knew of this power when he had his typesetter concretize certain passages in *Alice in Wonderland*, just as Guillaume Apollinaire understood when he devised his first *Calligrammes* (see page 10).

Talking type, while virtually as old as type itself, is never old hat. Accents may change from culture to culture, volume may be modulated from project to project, but type continues to speak at all levels. The Futurists' and Dadaists' typographic voices were loud; the Aestheticists' were quiet. With so many accents, dialects, and styles from which to choose, it is no wonder the contemporary murmur of typographic babble is getting louder. Paul Rand referred to the latest manifestation of talking type as "rap typography," literally suggesting the syncopation, rhythm, and rhyme found in rap music. In a broader sense, Rand meant that today's talking type can be improvisational like jazz, varied like a partite, or structured like a motet—expressive at best, nihilistic at worst.

Rap typography is not exclusively concerned with the approximation of sound, but takes many forms from onomatopoeic poems (à la Marinetti's *parole in liberta*) to the transparent and layered typographics referred to in today's design argot as "deconstruction." The sources of rap typography vary, and the technique cannot be pigeonholed merely as a humorous or stylistic conceit, though much of what is current is stylistic. Some designers are truly experimenting with relationships of form and meaning; others are just perpetuating a code. Recent advertisements for Nike shown here represent a synthesis of these two approaches into what has quickly become a popular typographic style, at once eye-catching and witty. Indeed, these ads and other manifestations indicate a type-as-art revival in youth-targeted advertising today.

Type Faces

Bradbury Thompson devotes a chapter of his book, *The Art of Graphic Design*, to "Type as Toy," which he defines as "graphic design conceived in the spirit of play and a sentiment for childhood." There can be no more obvious return to child's play

A haughty Solo logo by Greg Simpson and Seymour Chwast.

in graphic design than the making of faces from type and letterforms. These are puns in the truest sense, as they are substitutions of one form for another—in this case, the appropriate letter for a mouth, an ear, a nose, or hair. The practice dates back to the development of letterforms and is an efficient mnemonic device, for it speaks simultaneously in language and in symbol.

A type-face for the AIGA membership guide designed by Pentagram/New York.

Paula Scher's illustration is a comical confluence.

Word Play

Typography gives words texture, even allure, but make no mistake about it—without the right words, there can be no meaning. Similarly, rap music may be entertaining, but it is at its best when the lyrics conjure up meaningful mental pictures. And rhyme without content is like doo-wop—toe-tapping, knee-slapping, but soon tiresome. Although this book's introduction began with a discussion of graphic design as the marriage of word and image, most of the examples shown here lean toward visual solutions in which words are secondary, if used at all. This section brings graphic wit and design humor back full-circle to the word as the focus. In most cases, the design is secondary to the humorous headline and slogan. Nevertheless, these works offer a harmonious mix of type, image, and word.

This billboard, designed by John Seymour-Anderson and written by Mike Gibbs, is bound to attract attention, even if you don't believe in alien real estate.

If not for humor—
particularly
the uniqely life-
affirming
quality of
my work—
the misery and wickedness
of the world would
be unbearable.

James Victore

A GOOD SENSE OF
HUMOR
OR A QUICK WIT ALWAYS SEEMED LIKE
SIGNS OF INTELLIGENCE
TO ME, OR AT LEAST SIGNS OF BEING
KEENLY OBSERVANT.
I THINK
A SENSE OF IRONY
PUTS PEOPLE AT EASE, TOO.

Gail Anderson

Chapter

Why Humor?

The following designers were each asked to select a piece that they thought fulfilled their definition of witty and then answer the same set of questions. Although the work is quite diverse, the role and goal of humor is fairly constant.

James Victore

Brian Collins

Mark Fox

Gail Anderson

Jeffrey Keyton

Alex Isley

Rick Valicenti

Jelly: Miriam Bossard
  & Amy Unikewicz

Steven Guarnaccia

Seymour Chwast

Peter Buchanan-Smith

Charles Spencer Anderson

Christoph Niemann

Josh Gosfield

Mirko Ilic

Michael Bartalos

Daniel Pelavin

Stefan Sagmeister

Peter Girardi

Steven Heller

Scott Stowell

Robbie Conal

Number Seventeen:
  Bonnie Siegler
  & Emily Oberman

How to draw a chicken.

 James **Victore**

What makes this work witty?
This poster for Portfolio Center is not actually witty. To me "witty" implies a certain level of sophistication that I personally do not posses. I do think that this is possibly funny, though. Why is it funny? Probably, like all humor, because it is true.

Was it a conscious decision to be witty?
Um . . . yes?

Is there a hidden, or subconscious joke involved? If so, what?
There is never anything hidden or subconscious in any of my work. Never ever. Never. Or, at least I don't think so.

What is the virtue of wit or humor?
If not for humor—particularly the uniquely life-affirming quality of my work—the misery and wickedness of the world would be unbearable. Indeed, some days are so bleak that I stare into the black swirling heavens, shake my fists and demand to know how a just god could create a universe so filled with suffering and . . . What was the question again?

Why did you select this as your wittiest piece?
This was a completely random choice to include. So, so many of my works are so totally hilarious that it was hard to choose just one. In the end I had to use the "eenie-meenie" process. I use this process quite often.

Did the client appreciate the humor?
Did the client appreciate my humor? EVERYBODY appreciates my humor.

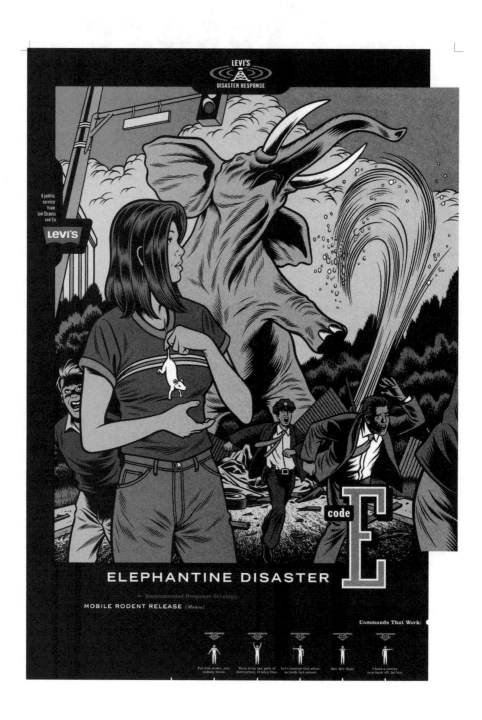

Brian **Collins**

℘roject:

LEVI STRAUSS & CO. DISASTER ALERT CAMPAIGN

What makes this work witty?

I am compelled to hold my tongue as wit is best judged by my audience. Not by me. All I will say is that people whom I believe to be charming have laughed at it.

Was it a conscious decision to be witty?

It was a conscious decision to be different. I was increasingly concerned by vulgar ads that celebrated binge and purge fashion models, especially when aimed at teenagers. I was also tired of the dull, commonplace photography being regurgitated across the category. Also, Levi's had not used illustration to advertise men's jeans in over a decade. I was also looking for an opportunity to work with comic artist Charles Burns. I guess my ambitions overlapped nicely.

Is there a hidden, or subconscious joke involved? If so, what?

This work was an attempt to comment on our culture's odd fascination with disasters. This work appeared in the season of violent movies like *Independence Day*, *Armageddon*, *Volcano*, *Deep Impact*, *Twister*, *Titanic*, *Godzilla*, etc. Scenes of people escaping exploding meteors, rampaging monsters, or killer windstorms had Americans lining up at the box office. I wanted to hijack that obsession—and warp it.

The idea was simple: If disaster strikes, Levi's would provide you with the information you need to survive: not to run away—but to stare the disaster down. So, when a meteor shower hits the planet, you would know how to use a handy baseball bat to smack the fiery little suckers back into outer space. (This campaign appeared one year before a Nike spot featured a celebrity baseball player doing the same thing with a meteorite, by the way.) Volcano? Marshmallow time. Tornado? Fly a kite. Elephant stampede? Grab a mouse—head for the trouble.

Simple.

We turned an entire west coast retail chain into Levi's Disaster Alert Stations. A cross between a fashion boutique and Civil Defense Shelter.

What is the virtue of wit or humor?

It subverts seriousness—the last refuge of the shallow.

Why did you select this as your wittiest piece?

Because it worked. Jeans sold. Kids liked them. They got the joke. And they stole the posters from the stores. I trust kids.

Did the client appreciate the humor?

My clients at Levi's got it and appreciated the project's comment on how disaster-obsessed our culture was at the time. And they believed posters worked great in the stores. Today though, so soon after the attacks on September 11, I couldn't present this as a worthy idea. Wit, evidently, can be time sensitive.

REPUBLICAN CONTRACT ON AMERICA

Bob Dole

Ralph Reed

Newt Gingrich

Rush Limbaugh

Bob Packwood

Jesse Helms

"When I hear anyone talk of culture,
I reach for my revolver."—Hermann Goering

Mark Fox

𝔓roject:

REPUBLICAN CONTRACT ON AMERICA

Silk screen on chip board (24" × 24", 1995)

What makes this work witty?
The Republicans and their much ballyhooed Contract with America are depicted as Mafia contract killers. The quote by Göering is used to highlight the anti-culture, anti-intellectual, anti-art stance of this Republican-controlled Congress.

Was it a conscious decision to be witty?
Yes. And absurd and obnoxious.

Is there a hidden joke?
Yes. Ralph Reed (former head of the Christian Coalition) controls the chamber; Newt Gingrich is the hammer; Bob Packwood—at the time under investigation for sexual misconduct—is the grip; Jesse Helms is the trigger. There is no sight.

What is the virtue of wit or humor?
Wit is the sugar that precedes the medicine.

Why did you select this piece?
This poster has historical value in that it responded to a particular moment—a rather divisive moment—in the political and cultural life of the nation. It is also of interest in that its edgy humor would be less welcome in this post-Timothy McVeigh, post-9/11 landscape.

Did the client appreciate the humor?
As the client, I loved this piece! Others seemed to be amused as well. This poster is part of the permanent design collection of the San Francisco Museum of Modern Art. It also appeared in the 1996 catalog for the exhibit "Mixing Messages," curated by Ellen Lupton at the Cooper-Hewitt in New York.

I gave a copy to President Clinton and he sent me a nice form letter back. It said "Thank you so much for your thoughtful gift. I am grateful for your generosity." I assured the president that no NEA funds were used to produce the poster.

Judges' Choices

Designers' Statements

Type
Directors
Club
Typeface
Design
Competition

TDC2

Winners

Gail **Anderson**

What makes this work witty?
Paint by number is just so warm and fuzzy. I think the homey, painted type is such a contrast to the crispy new fonts in the TDC2 section of the book that you just have to smile when you see it.

Was it a conscious decision to be witty?
I had hopes that the work would elicit a little chuckle here and there, so I guess it was a conscious decision to attempt humor. I think I was going for clever and then ended up at silly in places because I was having such a good time working on the Photoshop paintings.

Is there a hidden, or subconscious joke involved? If so, what?
I thought it would be fun to create some really earnest paint by number artwork, and render elaborate type on the section opener. If you're really paying attention, when you turn to the "unpainted canvas" spread, you'll see that I used letters, not numbers to indicate color. That's my little because-it's-the-TYPE Directors-Club joke. And the letters really correspond to the right colors, which means that I have a lot of free time on my hands.

What is the virtue of wit or humor?
A good sense of humor or a quick wit always seemed like signs of intelligence to me, or at least signs of being keenly observant. I think a sense of irony puts people at ease, too. The work that I've been proudest of usually has a little wink-wink in it some-where.

Why did you select this as your wittiest piece?
I think I actually pulled off what I was going for. Maybe because I'm actually happy with what I've done, I suddenly look at it as pretty darn clever. But if I look at the pages really hard, I'll find some fatal flaw. Then it'll go from witty straight to stupid.

Did the client appreciate the humor?
I think I came off as wittier than I am in real life, so it did its job.

Jeffrey **Keyton**

𝔓roject:

MTV VIDEO MUSIC AWARDS: BEST POP VIDEO

COPY: BEST POP VIDEO

OPEN: AHHHH! LOOK AT AL THOSE BOOBIES!

CLOSE: IF ONE BOOBY DOES IT, THE OTHERS FOLLOW.

What makes this work witty?

In this spot it's a combination of elements that makes for the wittiness. First there is the concept: a parody of nature documentaries. Second is the application of that to the MTV Video Music Awards nomination categories, which in this case was Best Pop Video. In the execution the main thrust of the humor lies simply in the word "booby," which is inherently funny. Finally, throw in a mature English accent for the voice over and it all adds up to one very witty spot.

Was it a conscious decision to be witty?

Yes it was a very conscious decision to be witty.

Is there a hidden, or subconscious joke involved? If so, what?

With the awards being held at an opera house we poked fun at the reserved and stuffy stereotypes of that world.

What is the virtue of wit or humor?

The virtue of wit . . . pleasure

Why did you select this as your wittiest piece?

I selected this piece simply because it is fresh in my mind. . . . I think one of the negatives of humor is that a joke can get tired quickly.

Did the client appreciate the humor?

The client loved the humor . . . . It would be a difficult pitch to make someone cry.

132

# Alex **Isley**

𝔓roject:

ANIMAL PLANET PRODUCT DEVELOPMENT AND IDENTITY PROGRAM

What makes this work witty?

This was an assignment for Animal Planet, a successful cable network. They hired us to help them introduce a new line of Animal Planet products into the marketplace. We established an editorial and visual approach for the products, producing a style guide that shows licensees not only how to implement the program but also how to convey the brand's spirit and sense of fun.

We established the idea that "animals are people, too," and set out to give personalities to the animals. We developed thought balloon devices, called Animusings, in order to let the animals inject some spirit and personality into the way the toys and clothing were created and merchandised. The cover of the style guide has a chimp thinking, "Hmm . . . should the logo be bigger?" This pretty much sets the tone of the whole program, and for some reason seems to strike a chord with those who must get their designs approved by management.

As part of our participation, we have written and designed packaging for over 150 products. What I'm most happy with is not so much the look we developed, but the spirit that comes across through the combination of text and imagery. A T-Rex thinks, "Boy, something extincts in here!" and a hippo asks, "Does this box make me look fat?".

Okay, maybe I'm the only one who thinks they are funny. The program has become very successful, however, and that is an encouragement.

Was it a conscious decision to be witty?

There was a conscious decision to give spirit and personality to the products. The idea of using humor came from that.

Is there a hidden, or subconscious joke involved? If so, what?

I don't think there's too much that's hidden here. This program relies exclusively on the power of the single entendre.

What is the virtue of wit or humor?

As it relates to marketing and graphic design, I think the power of humor lies in that people tend to remember things that amuse them. While I've read King Lear, I can't remember enough to quote from it. But I can recite for you the entire dialogue

from the Minister of Silly Walks. I think that amusing things just stick in people's heads a little better. And that's certainly a goal when you're out to create effective communication.

Of course, you probably shouldn't try to make everything funny. See below.

Why did you select this as your wittiest piece?

Over the years, fortunately or not, my firm has been associated with "funny" clients. On the downside, this can sometimes scare off potential clients with "straighter" assignments, but at the end of the day I'm fortunate to have had the experience of working with the editors of the much-missed *Spy* magazine, being punched on the arm by "the usual gang of idiots" at *Mad,* and doing work that emphasizes kids' noisy bodily functions for Nickelodeon. The smarter clients realize that we tailor our solutions to the audience and to the goals of the assignments. We're not always funny, but we try to always be smart about things.

If you're doing work for "funny" clients, it's pretty much expected that your design needs to incorporate humor. But it's also pretty easy to do that, as you're working with material that is typically funny by itself. Actually, I've found that in these cases, the challenge for the designer is to not screw things up by unduly goofyfying the work. It's a trap that I think we fall into quite often; you can usually see when someone's designing for a kid or a "funny" client by the way they tilt the photos at wacky angles or use zany typefaces.

That seems pretty lazy to me. It's like starting off a joke by saying "This is really funny . . . ."

As the editors of Spy used to say, a joke is funnier when told by a guy in a tuxedo than in a clown suit.

Anyway, what I've chosen to show here is a situation in which humor was not required or expected, but by taking a more lighthearted approach we made the work more effective.

Did the client appreciate the humor?

Yes. Not only that, we have been told by many people in the industry that the success of the approach we took for Animal Planet has influenced the development of similar brand extensions for other properties, and demonstrated how this type of program can work. The sales have been impressive. I think the client appreciates that even more than humor.

Rick **Valicenti**

What makes this work witty?
Timing is everything . . . but the unexpected juxtaposition is always a refreshing pie-in-the-face! The context was for a FLUXUS retrospective poster at the Arts Club of Chicago. The budget was low and the relevance high. I thought this was in the Fluxus spirit. They didn't. We settled for the Coppertone Girl being ravaged by security dog imagery from the yellow pages . . . . The headline was, "Relax, the average life span is 2 billion seconds."

Was it a conscious decision to be witty?
It more a conscious decision to make the comment, "what da fuck . . . life goes on," or, "display unbridled zeal" . . . "whichever does it for you!"

Is there a hidden, or subconscious joke involved?
Imagine if Jimi lived long enough to play Vegas . . . what kind of art would that have been.

What is the virtue of wit or humor?
Come on, Steve . . .

Okay, okay, from where I stand, humor is a fine example of generosity from one person to another. It triggers a moment of pure delight and joy. Like fine art, fine wine, a good idea, an insight, good sex, a passionate kiss, maternal comfort on a sick day, a free drink when you are thirsty, a fanny pat from the coach upon a job well done, applause from the crowd, and etc. . . . humor ranks up there with all of above and then some.

Why did you select this as your wittiest piece?
I thought you would like it.

Did the client appreciate the humor?
No . . . Did I appreciate the humor? You betcha, and that's all that matters to me.

Jelly:

Miriam Bossard & Amy Unikewicz

Project:

HOLIDAY GREETING CARD

Would you provide a brief explanation of this piece?
The portrait of us, disguised as Heinzelmaennchen, was originally intended to appear on the contributors page of *Swissair Gazette*, the in-flight magazine of Swissair, as a credit for our redesign of the magazine. Intended as a subtle comment on the extremely tight deadline in which we had to do our work, the Heinzelmaennchen costumes refer to a popular Swiss and German fairytale featuring the fairies that come out at night, work miraculously fast and, by morning, have taken care of everything in the best possible way.

Swissair Gazette, however, refused to print this version of our portrait, asking that we supply instead something more discrete. Their rationale was that nobody would pay attention to the other contributors on the page, because our portrait would be overshadowing theirs.

We then resurrected our abandoned Heinzelmaennchen for the New Year's card, sprinkling some magic glitter, some holiday charm and a message for good fortune— in hopes of bringing new clients and interesting miracle work in 2002.

What makes this work witty?
It's businesswomen in hooded dwarf outfits!

Was it a conscious decision to be witty?
It was much more a light-hearted, cheeky approach to not taking the portrait thing so seriously.

Is there a hidden, or subconscious joke involved? If so, what?
For Europeans and friends in the know, its subtle reference to the Heinzelmaennchen is pretty funny.

What is the virtue of wit or humor?
Wit and humor are beautiful because they touch on shared experiences: Common knowledge or common sense make someone able to understand why something is witty. They allow us to communicate difficult or complex messages in an easy, digestible way, offering a new context and therefore a more objective view on matters.

Why did you select this as your wittiest piece?
Because it represents the kind of humor that colors our studio philosophy.

Did the client appreciate the humor?
See answer above. However, as a holiday card the response has been delightful!

Steven **Guarnaccia**

Project:
POSTCARD

What makes this work witty?
The humor's in the signage overkill, and the fact that all the signs, in one way or another, say the same thing. And the more verbose the sign, the funnier ("Caution Entryway Approaching on Right," i.e.). "This is Not an Exit," you kind of have to translate, out of the negative, which gives it an element of surprise. Also, the speaker's word balloon, the butt of the joke, functions visually as another "sign."

Was it a conscious decision to be witty?
Yeah, I pretty much approach all assignments from a humorous perspective, especially if it's a straight piece I'm called on to illustrate. In this instance, the assignment was simply to illustrate the word "in."

Is there a hidden, or subconscious joke involved? If so, what?
There is one "inside" joke, for the connoisseur. The arrow on the ground, "This Way to the Ingress," echoes a sign Barnum put up in his museum that said, "This Way to the Egress." Though it sounded like he was leading people to the next attraction, "egress" just means "exit."

What is the virtue of wit or humor?
Don't get me started. I believe wit and humor keep the world humming along on its axis. Less grandly, they also convey ideas in a very smooth way. I think humor is one of those fast-acting transparent delivery systems that eases the concept to the brain. It's absorbed seemingly effortlessly and gives great pleasure, at the same time.

Why did you select this as your wittiest piece?
I picked this piece because it still makes me laugh whenever I look at it, which I can't say for a lot of my work. This is partly due, I think, to the fact that this is a situational gag—the little guy with the hat is a funny guy in a funny situation. He's clueless in a world where the clues are written large and clear.

Did the client appreciate the humor?
The client did, but then clients tend to come to me for humor in the first place, so it's never a hard sell, thank goodness.

✵THE KAMA SUTRA of READING✵

THE FLOWER.
THE MALE BOOK LOVER READS A HOW-TO BOOK ON HIS BACK WHILE SHE LEANS ON HIM AND LISTENS.

THE ORIGINAL MANUAL OF LOVE MAKING, WRITTEN ALMOST 2000 YEARS AGO BY VATSYAYANA HAS BEEN ADAPTED FOR THE MODERN READER. PAINSTAKING RESEARCH AND EXPERIMENTATION HAVE RESULTED IN THE FOLLOWING EXAMPLES DESIGNED FOR THE MOST PLEASURABLE READING EXPERIENCES.

THE COBRA.
BOOK LOVERS WHO HAVE BEEN ARGUING MAY FIND RELIEF IN THIS BACK-TO-BACK PO-SITION. LIGHT READING IS PREFERRED.

THE INVERTED COW.
HE IS ON HIS ELBOWS AND KNEES. SHE RESTS ON HIS BAGAVITA. THEY READ SHORT FICTION.

THE SCISSORS.
STANDING BACK TO BACK 3 FEET APART, OUR BOOK LOVERS LEAN ON EACH OTHER. BEST ARE BOOKS ON POPULAR PSYCHOLOGY.

THE SWASTIKA.
HE RESTS HIS BODY ON HIS ELBOWS WHILE SHE READS BETWEEN HIS LEGS. NON FICTION IS RECOMMENDED.

THE CRAB. OUR BOOK LOVERS SIT UPRIGHT FACING EACH OTHER. EACH RESTS ONE LEG ON THE OTHER'S KNEE. GOTHIC NOVELS ARE BEST.

THE TRAIN. THE WOMAN SITS BETWEEN THE LEGS OF THE MAN. HE READS TRAVEL BOOKS TO HER.

S. CHWAST.

142

Seymour **Chwast**

KAMA SUTRA COMIC STRIP FOR THE *NEW YORK TIMES BOOK REVIEW*

What makes this work witty?
The Kama Sutra is a serious Indian guidebook for sex partners. It is explicit in explaining proper positions and giving these positions absurd names. (Sex can easily evoke giggles.) To apply these positions to the mundane activity of reading, in a mock serious manner, is incongruous and funny.

Was it a conscious decision to be witty?
Yes.

Is there a hidden, or subconscious joke involved? If so, what?
I hope not. I want everybody to get it.

What is the virtue of wit or humor?
Humor is relief from the anxiety that the human condition generates. It is also an opportunity to attack pomposity in who we are and what we do.

Why did you select this as your wittiest piece?
I picked the piece because of its straight-faced silliness.

Did the client appreciate the humor?
I suggest you ask Steve Heller.

Dear Mets Fans,

How to get to Babe's House:

Enter subway at Willets Point-Shea Stadium.
Get on westbound No. 7 train.
Take train to Grand Central Station.
When you come to a fork in the road, take it.
Get on uptown No. 4 train.
Take train to 161st street-Yankee Stadium.

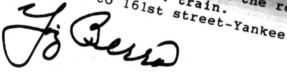

p.s. It's not too far-
     it just seems like it is.

Peter Buchanan-Smith

Project:

YOGI BERRA FOR THE NEW YORK TIMES OP-ED PAGE

What makes this work witty?

This piece ran the day after the Mets and Yankees had just advanced through the first two playoff rounds to reach the much awaited 2000 Subway Series. The idea came to me at 2:00 P.M. on a Friday, which left me with six hours to hand in a finished piece. I called all sorts of famous New Yorkers, none of them were willing to participate (although Guiliani's press secretary said it was a cute idea). After a few strokes of good luck, I found myself talking to Yogi Berra's son (who was with Yogi) on the twelfth hole somewhere in New Jersey. I ran the idea by him, told him what I wanted it to say, he was game, and we were off to the races.

It's a funny piece because it's art by Yogi Berra. Op-arts are usually reserved for so-called professional artists, illustrators and photographers. To ask a baseball player to create something—let alone Yogi (an artist in his own right)—is funny. We tend to think of Yogi as a Yankee, but he spent some time with the Mets: So if anyone knew how to get to Babe's house from Shea stadium, it was him. So on the outset, this piece poses as being practical: which is funny because any Met fan in his right mind knows how to get to the Stadium.

Was it a conscious decision to be witty?

It was initially meant to be witty, but became wittier when Yogi got on board. His willingness to play ball with us was so inspiring that it enhanced the copy and the design.

Why did you select this as your wittiest piece?

Because I can't draw, I depend on good concepts. Not only was this piece funny, but it was also a successful concept: concepts being the nuts and bolts of the op-ed page. Although I didn't get the byline, it was my baby.

Did the client appreciate the humor?

The Yogi Berra museum took four copies for their archives and the *Times* made a donation to his charity, my editors couldn't believe that I had pulled off such a stunt, and the Yankees won the World Series. What could be better?

Charles Spencer
Anderson

Project:

THE "NOUVEAU SALON DES CENT" AT THE CENTRE POMPIDOU
(ANNIVERSARY OF THE DEATH OF TOULOUSE-LAUTREC POSTER)

What makes this work witty?

I'm not really sure any of our work fits into the witty category. Perhaps funny. Witty seems more like humor deftly applied with a dose of intelligence. We try to stay away from that sort of thing.

Was it a conscious decision to be witty?

I'm not sure if it actually is witty (not to mention pretty or wise).

Is there a hidden or subconscious joke involved?

No, it's a pretty blatant and conscious joke, but with an underlying grain of truth veiled in sarcasm.

What is the virtue of wit or humor?

The use of humor allows corporate clients to maximize their synergistic paradigms in regard to corporate communications.

Why did you select this as your wittiest piece?

I selected it as a funny piece (I thought witty was optional). For additional thoughts on witty, see above.

Did the client appreciate the humor?

He's probably spinning in his grave.

FURNITURE — PORN

XXX!!! WATCH THEM DO IT ALL!!! XXX!!! XXX!!! XXX!!! ADULTS ONLY!!!XXX

Christoph **Niemann**

𝔓roject:

COMIC WEB SITES

What makes this work witty?

The assignment was to do the ten least visited Web sites ever (this is one of them).
The problem was of course that there is every possible insanity out there on the Web
already. That's why I thought it was funny to show something as bland as a chair and
a table and present it as something outrageous.

Was it a conscious decision to be witty?

Yes.

Is there a hidden, or subconscious joke involved? If so, what?

Not that I am aware of.

What is the virtue of wit or humor?

I guess the way witty design works is that it usually is like a little riddle that the reader has to solve. Hence, it almost gets an interactive quality, because, unlike with
purely formal design, the reader cannot only consume the design, but has to think to
make it work.

Why did you select this as your wittiest piece?

I do not think I can judge my own work, therefore I am not 100 percent sure this is
my single wittiest work ever. I simply like it.

Did the client appreciate the humor?

In this case, it was pretty clear from the assignment that the client was looking for
something funny. Since they paid me and printed the piece, I assume that they appreciated it.

Josh **Gosfield**

𝔓roject:

BUSH AND GORE TOYS

What makes this work witty?

Portraying the two jokers of the 2000 presidential election in guises that reflected and exaggerated their foolishness. Bush is shown as the cheap huckster, hawking the same tired bill of goods that his daddy sold. Gore is the stiff robotic hunk of metal incapable of expressing a shred of humanity.

Was it a conscious decision to be witty?

Yes, because the whole election fiasco was so depressing. It was in the time-honored tradition of laughing to keep from crying.

Is there a hidden, or subconscious joke involved? If so, what?

Nothing subconscious. I'm too simple for that.

What is the virtue of wit or humor?

Telling a story with humor can disarm the viewer. This allows the artist to show his emotional or symbolic truth that might not be entirely factual. Like dreams of psychotic delusions, it's a chance to elude the clutches of the logical mind, and deliver the information to a nonrational part of the brain.

Why did you select this as your wittiest piece?

By virtue of being my most recent piece, it strikes me as the funniest. Tomorrow's will seem even funnier.

Did the client appreciate the humor?

Yes. The clients, Richard Press and Eden Lipson of *Times Talk* were fully on board with this approach. In fact the idea was as much Richard Press's as mine. Way before the assignment, Richard and I had spent a lot of time bemoaning the sad state of the 2000 election.

Mirko Ilic

What makes this work witty?

One doesn't expect hotel ephemera to be funny. It's usually serious and often pretentious. Since the guests of the hotel must receive these things anyway, I decided to go beyond that. How many times do you smile at a laundry bag, or the slip that holds it?

Was it a conscious decision to be witty?

New York hotel rooms are small, with few items in them. I wanted to pay attention to these things.

Is there a hidden, or subconscious joke involved? If so, what?

It began with the logo. The hotel is in Times Square, with small rooms, each with a primary color theme: red, yellow, or blue. The square in the logo sits in the H, so you have reference to Times Square, the little red rooms inside the hotel, and to "H," the international symbol for hotel. All other items played off of this.

What is the virtue of wit or humor?

Whenever you see females interviewed on television, they are asked of the most important quality in a man. Usually, they say "sense of humor." Then they walk into the sunset with a rich, boring guy.

Why did you select this as your wittiest piece?

It is easier to be witty on the cover of intelligent magazines, harder to do so on utilitarian things like annual reports or fax cover sheets.

Did the client appreciate the humor?

Yes, they laughed all the way to the bank. They must have liked it, or would not have allowed it to be printed.

Michael **Bartalos**

What makes this work witty?
An unorthodox approach to stamp design and the addition of winged feet to the marathon runner.

Was it a conscious decision to be witty?
Yes, the stamp was meant to have a "twist" and element of surprise.

Is there a hidden, or subconscious joke involved? If so, what?
A close look reveals the marathoner sporting a pair of winged feet, an allusion to the fleet-footed Greek god Hermes and the Hellenic origins of the sport.

What is the virtue of wit or humor?
The virtue of humor is that it engages us by appealing to our emotions. Ideas that make us laugh tend to communicate messages effectively and memorably. My humor attempts to communicate ideas on various levels, mainly through metaphor, exaggeration, or unexpected and incongruous imagery.

Why did you select this as your wittiest piece?
The fantasy element and unexpected allusion to history in this image amused me. I was pleased to bring more substance to this postage stamp than a simple straight-forward image of a Marathon runner.

Did the client appreciate the humor?
Very much so. I was told that its humorous approach was what sold the Stamp Advisory Committee on this design.

Daniel Pelavin

What makes this work witty?
It is a parody of a familiar genre (i.e., the matchbook ad) applied to the unlikely subject of typesetting.

Was it a conscious decision to be witty?
It was intended to amuse.

Is there a hidden, or subconscious joke involved? If so, what?
The "joke" is that the actual ad would have read "You have Bad Breath . . ." an embarrassing situation but one that makes a designer's obsession over the quality of his typography seem a little silly and perhaps vain.

What is the virtue of wit or humor?
To capture attention and leave a memorable impression.

Why did you select this as your wittiest piece?
It was done in the days before I decided that wit did more to limit the success of a communication than it did to enhance it.

Did the client appreciate the humor?
The client laughed so hard he began to cough and nearly wet himself and then had the piece mounted in a specially constructed frame and mounted it on the wall of his studio.

Stefan Sagmeister

Project:

AIGA POSTER

What makes this work witty?
I am not sure: Are speaker names and self-portraits drawn on Avery labels witty? Is a chicken running around with no head witty?

Was it a conscious decision to be witty?
No. The AIGA had just sent such a massive amount of copy over to be featured on the back of the poster that, after trying the information architecture thing with color coding and thick and thin bars, we gave up and just placed the copy wherevereach-way. Some tiny spaces remained empty and we added our own copy like this little story my printer told me: So, my printer in New Jersey works on this very large job for a fancy food fair in New Orleans. His client is the market leader in that segment, a magazine called "Frozen Vegetables." It was a rush job, they had worked several night shifts to get a special fancy food fair issue down to New Orleans in time for the show opening on Friday. The magazines (lots and lots of boxes) were delivered by courier to the hotel where the client stayed. But the boxes could not be found. The courier company had a delivery signature that was unreadable. Friday's show opening: No Magazines. Saturday: No Magazines. These guys had ten people down there to man the stand and no magazines anywhere. They had to go home without giving ONE magazine away. Two weeks later they found them in the walk-in refrigerator of the hotel. The boxes were labeled: "Frozen Vegetables."

Is there a hidden, or subconscious joke involved? If so, what?
We had just photographed my testicles for another project, so I had a Polaroid of that photo shoot lying around, which fit beautifully into one of those empty spaces. Wrote a little story next to it pretending it represents a monkeys knee. Nobody objected.

What is the virtue of wit or humor?
To entice a smile, to involve the viewer.

Why did you select this as your wittiest piece?
Cause I'm a witless nitwit.

Did the client appreciate the humor?
Yes, they were great about it, even when complaints from AIGA members came in (the notice to animal friends promising no chickens were harmed in the making of this poster—apart from some delicious Chicken McNuggets we enjoyed while Photoshopping) drew the most nasty calls.

Peter **Girardi**

What makes this work witty?
I don't know if it's exactly witty. Some people might think so. It's more funny in a sort of vulgar fashion.

Was it a conscious decision to be witty?
No. Consciously witty work I always find boring.

Is there a hidden, or subconscious joke involved? If so, what?
Not at all. Nothing subconscious here. Just flat out funny.

What is the virtue of wit or humor?
The virtue of Humor? Keeping sane in an inane world.

Why did you select this as your wittiest piece?
It's one of the more funnier pieces we've done. It all works together well. The animation style is appropriate for the humor.

Did the client appreciate the humor?
We were the client and we cracked ourselves up.

The New York Times

April 4, 1999 $1.25

Book Review

Copyright © 1999 The New York Times

The News This Year Oh Boy!

A lucky President made the grade, with a little help from his enemies and even his friends. Which was George Stephanopoulos? Garry Wills looks into that **4** Tom Goldstein reviews Michael Isikoff's 'Uncovering Clinton' **5** And Michael Oreskes examines 'Monica's Story,' by Andrew Morton **6**

Steven **Heller**

𝔓roject:

SGT. CLINTON'S LONELY HEARTS CLUB BAND, ILLUSTRATED BY ED LAM

What makes this work witty?
I couldn't resist answering my own questions. Particularly because I'm not very funny and rely on others to be funny for me. So, with that as a preamble, this is funny because of context. It is a parody of the famous Sgt. Pepper album, which has been parodied up the whazoo. While I try to stay away from clichés, this was too good to pass up, ready made for the Clinton era.

Was it a conscious decision to be witty?
Of course it was a conscious decision, and one that I hoped would not embarrass myself. It illustrated a collection of books about the Clinton presidency, including his fabled misadventures. This idea was ideal, ready made to encapsulate the entire escapade. I just needed a great artist to render it. Ed Lam was perfect. What's more, the idea would have been limp if not for his contributions. He not only did a perfect rendering, he gave all characters the conceptual foundation necessary to make it funny—and take it to the next step of wit.

Is there a hidden, or subconscious joke involved? If so, what?
There is nothing subconscious because to be funny it must be overt. But, there are little hidden gems throughout the art in the same sense as the original Sgt. Pepper album. One can spend hours trying to figure out what's what and who's who.

What is the virtue of wit or humor?
Well, parody is a form of wit and humor that forces recognition. When it works, it exaggerates the unique characteristics (sometimes flaws) of the object being parodied. In this case, it became something of an icon—or signpost of the Clinton era.

Why did you select this as your wittiest piece?
It is my wittiest piece as an art director because it is such a pure idea married to the right artist. It could have failed at any point. It could have been overdone, underdone, or just plain stupid. But it worked, thanks mostly to the skill of the artist, not me.

Did the client appreciate the humor?
Well, I'm the client, and I loved what Ed Lam produced. My editor was pleased, too. But I never heard from Bill or Hillary. That was disappointing. Often I'll get a call from the author or subject of a book asking to buy the art. I know Ed got calls, but neither from the president nor the Beatles.

164

Peter **Blegvad**

𝔓roject:

LEVIATHAN COMIC STRIP

What makes this work witty?

Redundancy, brevity, sound effects. The clash of static fact and symbolic motion. The contrast between the sanity of the drawing—the technical precision of the locomotive (taken from a Dover book) and the detailed cat (taken from Victorian illustrator, Ernest Grisset)—and the lunatic dialogue.

Was it a conscious decision to be witty?

Yes. I put the image together first and then agonized over the caption.

Is there a hidden, or subconscious joke involved? If so, what?

I don't know if it's strictly a joke, but the secret agenda, the regressive mission of this cartoon is to destroy the world. Or at least to blur the border between the imaginary and the real. To elevate the imaginary to the status of the real.

What is the virtue of wit or humor?

It's revenge. It's life against death. It's rejuvenating. Humor distracts the dominant half of the brain (bureaucratic) so that the other half (ludic, poetic, oneiric) is engaged. Suddenly we think in stereo. Humor makes us look twice, so that instead of merely recognizing we see.

Why did you select this as your wittiest piece?

For its simplicity.

Did the client appreciate the humor?

Leviathan ran for seven-and-a-half years in *The Independent on Sunday*. The editors didn't say much, but they kept running it, which I interpreted as appreciation.

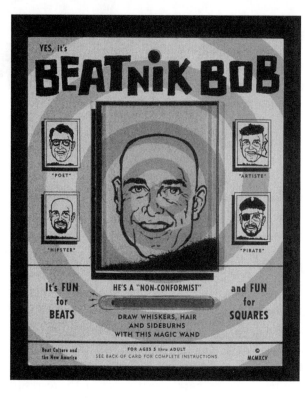

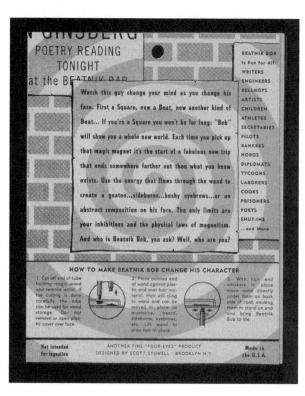

Scott **Stowell**

What makes this work witty?

A few years back, I got the project to create products to accompany the "Beat Culture in the New America" show at the Whitney Museum. Besides the obligatory mug, T-shirt and mouse-pad, I developed some products which were less literal and more based on the concepts behind Beat culture. One product was a box of pencils called "Tools for Modern Prose" (*www.notclosed.com/pages/pencils.html*) based on a piece by Jack Kerouac. Another was the project: Beatnik Bob. This product was a custom version of the old "Wooly Willy" toy, which contains metal filings you can move with a magnetic stylus to create various configurations of facial hair. This version uses the same physical toy as the original, but I created all-new artwork and copy—except the "not intended for ingestion" warning. That was on the original toy and was already pretty funny. I kept the original instructions as well. The idea here was to address the pop-culture reaction to the Beats—pulp novels, movie posters, advertising—by having the Whitney produce and sell a parody of those things. Also, the idea of changing one's identity related well to the freedom and escapism that the Beats epitomized to so many people. And it's fun to play with. Plus, there's a pirate on it. Pirates are funny.

Was it a conscious decision to be witty?

Yes.

Is there a hidden, or subconscious joke involved? If so, what?

No.

What is the virtue of wit or humor?

It's surprising, disarming, and human. Humor is the best way to make people think about things they hadn't planned on thinking about—it's a way of confronting and avoiding ideas at the same time. Plus, people like to laugh—they can't help it.

Why did you select this as your wittiest piece?

I wouldn't necessarily call it my wittiest piece, as I often try to be witty without being actually funny. This is a piece that is actually trying to be funny.

Did the client appreciate the humor?

Yes. The Whitney loved it. Regular people loved it. However, Allen Ginsberg was seen playing with one at the exhibition opening, and he was not happy—apparently he felt that it didn't take the Beats seriously enough. Oh well.

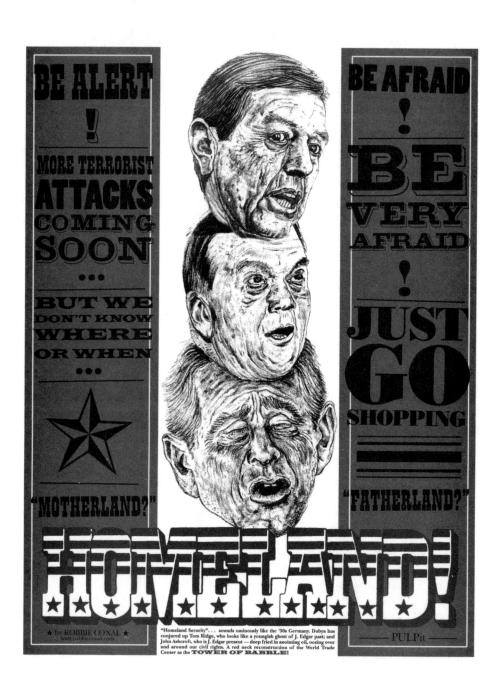

BE ALERT
!
MORE TERRORIST
ATTACKS
COMING
SOON
...
BUT WE
DON'T KNOW
WHERE
OR WHEN
...

"MOTHERLAND?"

BE AFRAID
!
BE
VERY
AFRAID
!
JUST
GO
SHOPPING

"FATHERLAND?"

HOMELAND!

★ by ROBBIE CONAL ★
www.robbieconal.com

"Homeland Security"... sounds ominously like the '30s Germany. Dubya has conjured up Tom Ridge, who looks like a youngish ghost of J. Edgar past; and John Ashcroft, who is J. Edgar present — deep fried in anointing oil, oozing over and around our civil rights. A red neck reconstruction of the World Trade Center as the TOWER OF BABBLE!

—PULPit—

Robbie Conal

Project:

HOMELAND POSTER

What makes this work witty?
If it's witty, it's out of exasperation, because there's nothing funny about it.

Was it a conscious decision to be witty?
It's all I've got. When humor is used as a defensive weapon—usually against a more powerful adversary—it becomes irony. When things look bleak and then get worse, it turns *black*. When there's no hope and it's just between you and it, you're at wit's end: it's just cathartic (usually accompanied by a most uncomfortable burning sensation). The major reason to make art like this is to go, "He-he-he, this'll be cool and when people see it, they'll wonder what the hell it is and how it got there."

Is there a hidden, or subconscious joke involved? If so, what?
One can only hope so. I, however, have no access to what it might be. I just know it's on me.

What is the virtue of wit or humor?
It makes all the pills easier to swallow.

Why did you select this as your wittiest piece?
I didn't. You did.

Did the client appreciate the humor?
I got paid my usual meager sum. I don't do it for the money (though I'll take all I can get); I do it because I can't bear not to.

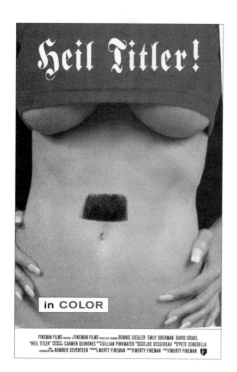

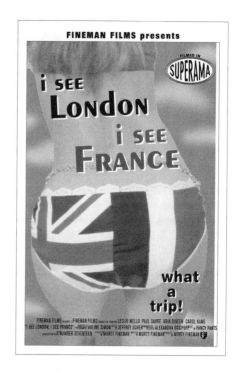

Number **Seventeen:**

Bonnie Siegler & Emily Oberman

Project:
MOVIE PARODIES

What makes this work witty?
We were lucky, because the client was witty, so before we even began working, we were already laughing at the titles we were given. Each one is a perfect parody in and of itself and we just tried to do the same thing visually.

Was it a conscious decision to be witty?
But, of course. Not just witty, either: down right silly, stupid, funny. In fact, everyone in the office did sketches for this job and the winning design was the one that got the most laughs from all of us.

Is there a hidden, or subconscious joke involved? If so, what?
Hopefully, the jokes are where everyone can see them, but we did put our names, and those of our friends and those of our pets in the credit blocks of each poster.

What is the virtue of wit or humor?
It makes you feel good all over and glad to be alive.

Why did you select this as your wittiest piece?
Because it consistently makes people laugh. Hard.

Did the client appreciate the humor?
Yes.

A ~~Couple of~~
three
Designers Talkin'
'Bout Humor

Michael Patrick Cronan designed a happy, alien-looking TV logo for TIVO.

Michael Patrick **Cronan**

on "HUMORS"

How would you define humor?

Latin defines humor as "fluid." In the middle ages "humors" referred to the fluids of the body. Being in a "bad humor" actually meant that you had a malady. The reference is still relevant if you consider that a "fluid" situation is one that contains unpredictable change.

It has been said many times that the basis of humor is pain or sadness. I would say that a more accurate statement would be that it's based on unexpected change. Change in the ancient world was synonymous with bad happenings. War, plague, drought are all changes that brought misery. Essentially, humor is a way to deal with the unexpected. A way to experience confusion without the bad consequences. It is also a way of seeing something from a new perspective. That makes it creative.

How, then, would you define graphic design humor?

Some humor must be visual. The sight gag without sight is not funny. Graphic design is a terrific way to present something funny. Graphics are great for comparing, explaining, or even exaggerating.

What makes design funny?

Intrinsically the arrangement of elements, typography and color is not very funny. A concept must start funny and then it becomes exaggerated and hopefully made funnier using the cunning of the designer.

Michael Patrick Cronan designed a series of image and word plays (this and following pages) used as free-standing art in major corporate conference rooms prior to the era of infectious greed.

Is being funny the quintessence of graphic humor, or is there some other, more subtle attribute?

I think there are many dimensions to humor and subtlety is one diminution that graphics captures. The drawings and paintings of Bruce McCall, for example, are visual humor that work on a number of levels. McCall creates images that are far fetched yet somehow sync up with how many of us would like the world to be. He once created a series of paintings of cars from the late Forties and early Fifties. The drivers and passengers were impossibly small inside the cars, giving the cars a heroic proportion. As it turns out, advertising from the era depicts the people in the cars

very much like McCall does. His people were very slightly smaller. So the humor not only spoofs the cars but also the advertising and in a way we are spoofed as well because we all understand the ideal and how we are manipulated as consumers.

What is the most humorous piece of graphic design you have ever seen?
I think the early ZAP comics containing the work of Robert Crumb is the funniest for me.

What is the most humorous piece of graphic design that you have ever done?
The Adaptec Annual Report is probably the most humorous piece we've done. Adaptec is a high-tech connector company. We created and photographed a pseudo-antique folk art collection using components that they manufacture. The joke is maintained throughout the book, including the financials and in fact the pieces are in plastic cases in their headquarters.

Can humor be taught?
I think humor can be taught. I still believe it is true that to become a graphic design-er one must have a well-developed sense of humor.

Michael Patrick Cronan designed a series of folk art pieces for the Adeptec annual report.

$700.50
AMERICA'S ONLY REMAINING OFF-LINE GRAPHIC DESIGN MAGAZINE,
now incorporating COMMUNICATION ARTS, METROPOLIS, STEP-BY-STEP, GRAPHIS, & EMIGRE
NOVEMBER/DECEMBER 2000
PRINT LV·VI

Print

MILLENNIUM ISSUE

Michael Dooley's parody of design magazines (this and following pages), including Print, Communication Arts, and Emigre, which appeared in the 1994 Print magazine self-parody issue.

Michael **Dooley**

How would you define humor?

I would define humor as the quick colorful insight that jumps over the lazy white set of expectations. But maybe that's just me.

How would you then define graphic design humor?

That would be the "billable" quick colorful insight that jumps over the lazy white, etc.

What makes design funny?

The most accurate gauges of funny design are the "Cleverness" to "Client Sense of Humor" inverse proportion ratio, and its corollary, "Everyone Here at the Agency Thought It Was Hilarious" to "Our Target Market Will Never Get It."

Is funny the quintessence of graphic humor, or is there some other attribute?

Funny you should ask. Stop me if you've heard this one before. Comedy is easy, revelatory, comedy is hard. If we're after the heart of transcendent graphic humor, we should listen for a resonance beyond the simple reflexive chuckle.

Take George Lois. Please! His shocking *Esquire* cover of My Lai's Lieutenant Calley—with deadly eyes and an Alfred E Newman grin, comfortably surrounded by haunted-looking Asian children—gives lie to the implicit mutual exclusiveness of the maxim, "That's not funny, that's sick." More significantly, the photo, taken by Carl Fischer, achieves a poignant, visceral truth.

Thanks so much. You've been a wonderful oil painting. Be sure to tip over your sacred cow on your way out.

What is the most humorous piece of graphic design you have ever seen?

Several of Art Spiegelman's works—the *Raw* magazine covers, the "Don't Get Around Much Anymore," and "Two-Fisted Painters" strips—have been quite memorable, but my favorite is his eight-page "Ace Hole, Midget Detective." It's certainly not laugh-out-loud humorous; in fact, in places it becomes downright downbeat. Nor is it a masterpiece of illustration; Spiegelman's drawing skills are workmanlike at best. Nevertheless, it's a sharp, surreal tale chockablock with verbal and visual punning and philosophizing, and one that rewards repeated readings. As a bonus, it's also a richly detailed meditation on the nature of fine art, comics, humor, creativity, and more!

DAWN OTT

BY PATRICK BOYLEPPLATE

MÍLK
DONUTS

HOW TO LOSE POUNDS BY CONSUMING JUNK F__D

Modern Holes in Your Food

You'll feel satisfied with an **EL DOUNUTCO**

OTT IS HOT from the perspective of the new millennium, Dawn Ott may prove to be the most important designer of the past century. She is equally adept at corporate communications, posters, packaging, interactive advertising, annual reports, and trademarks, handling each project with flair and sophistication. Her multi-faceted skills and boundless energy have made her the most exciting phenomenon to rise to prominence since all those incredibly talented people we gushed over in "Clients Who Sleep with Designers" and all the other feature articles in our last issue.

The public has responded to Ott's designs with overwhelming enthusiasm. Judges of every major competition lavish her with awards. And her clients—an international roster that includes many Fortune 500 corporations—love her work. The work itself represents a major breakthrough in an era oversaturated with high-tech visuals. As the print media has become all but obsolete, Ott manages to evoke a purer, pre-digitized period while embodying a contemporaneity that is truly of-the-moment. In summary, her designs are successful because they blend a modernistic simplicity with a post-avant-retro-neo-deconstructivist something-or-other.

Insert career history here

Ott began her professional career at Leo Burnett in Chicago, animating Poppin' Fresh for Pillsbury commercials. Anticipating the trend which shifted activity from major urban agencies to smaller regional services—also known as the Madison Avenue Crash of 1996—she returned to her hometown of Churros, New Mexico, six years ago and

established her own studio. After years of toil and struggle, she now enjoys her status as the profession's designer *du jour*.

At 45, Ott has flowing salt-and-pepper hair, sparkling maple syrup eyes, a cherry LifeSaver-sized circle tattoo on her left shoulder blade, and a spirit as effervescent as a glass of root beer freshly plopped with ice cream. I recently spoke with her for fifteen minutes at her comfortably cluttered studio as I grabbed a handful of projects to accompany this article.

Even more cloying superlatives

One of Ott's greatest strengths is that she continues to challenge herself, relishing the opportunity to experiment with different styles, techniques, and mediums. "If I wanted to spend my life following convenient formulas and producing superficial work, I'd be a writer for CA magazine," she explained candidly. "I'm happiest when I'm given creative latitude. The more freedom, the better. That way, I can continually explore my full potential to arrive at a unique yet appropriate solution that will please me as well as my client. But this is the same response you get from everyone you interview, shouldn't it be obvious to you by now?"

Speaking of obvious, at the risk of inducing cavities in the reader by dishing out another huge glob of puff-pastry praise, it's obvious to me that Ott will continue to please clients, and an increasingly receptive audience, well into the Twenty-first Century.

This page and right: Designs that Graphis magazine didn't want for their article on Dawn Ott.

a telephone conversation with . . . (Dawn)

conducted Friday, October 27, 2000, 12:30 PM

IGNORÉ

Dawn: Hello?

Rudy Dawn, it's Rudy VandzuZans calling from Emigre magazine.
D: [pause] You're still publishing Emigre?

R: Yes, and I was wondering if I could interview you.
D: Sure, go ahead.

R: First of all, I'd like to point out that all the other graphic design magazines are wasting valuable space talking about what a great designer you are and that all the other designers are wasting their talents imitating your style, but nobody is paying attention to your early work, such as your "Non-sense" poster, your Düngenheapen CD cover, and your designs for Ego magazine. I think that work is **unbelievably** brilliant and deserves more exposure.
D: I'm flattered you feel that way, but that work was done a long, long time ago.

R: But those designs are really amazing. They have an incredible passion to them, a vitality, a wonderful unpolished look.
D: Actually, they were very unpolished. I did them back when I was in preschool.

R: It doesn't matter that none of that work received any design awards. Anybody who can afford to pay all those entry fees can win awards. They're just an **unbelievably** big scam anyway. Those magazines and companies who run these contests just sit

This caption is supposed to identify the designs, but I merely got sloppy during the last stages of produc—

back and rake in the money. What they should do is go around the world themselves and look at everything that everybody is doing, and then pick the winners.
D: Rudy, I was just playing around. This work wasn't serious at all.

R: The fact that this work ignores all the rules shows that you were brave enough to treat graphic design as though it was fine art.

Why do designers always want graphic design to be graphic design?

DUNGHEAP
KISS MY HOLE

Why shouldn't graphic design be fine art? Then fine art can go on to be something else, like hatband fabric.
D: They ignore all rules because I was three-and-a-half years old when I made them. I didn't know anything about design. I didn't even know how to spell.

R: And the way this work defies legibility shows you don't care whether old people can read it? Who cares about old people anyway? People read best what they read most, and old people read the least. They just sit around reminiscing about how great Modernism was and losing their eyesight. They're so

hung unbelievably **up on**

outmoded concepts like grace and elegance that they can't appreciate funny-looking electronic fonts. They can't even appreciate funny-sounding music. So obviously they're not going to buy any of our mail-order merchandise.
D: Rudy, I just...

R: And this work also shows you're not afraid of being accused of self-indulgence. Critics always accuse me of being self-indulgent. What kind of nonsense is that? What do they want me to do? Indulge them? Who cares about critics? When our magazine had funny production quality and our typography had funny kerning, the critics said we were simply a passing fad. Now these same critics say we singlehandedly transformed the entire face of graphic design back then. Now these same critics say our relevance when the entire field became radicalized. They say I've fallen back on formula layouts so often that even David Carson's work is starting to look original. They say our new fonts look like cheap novelty items. They even say I've developed such a siege mentality I've become an émigré from

fuck my Boldly

will you eat me?

reality, the insane. But I simply don't care. Reality is that I will continue to be preoccupied with every stupid comment from people such as Massimo Vignelli

unbelievably throughout the next millennium if I want to

my magazine and...

R: Dawn? Are you still there?

Hello?

Hello?

What is the most humorous piece of graphic design that you have ever done?

My personal choice is a self-generated project I created for *Print* magazine's "Millennium Parody" issue. I started with the premise that six magazines—*Communication Arts*, *Metropolis*, *Step-by-Step*, *Graphis*, *Emigre*, and *Print* itself—would run feature spreads on the same graphic designer, Dawn Ott, a character I'd fabricated for the occasion. I then had the writers, whom I based on real people, view Ott through their own subjective-tinted lenses, each failing to recognize the obvious, fundamental fact that all her creations were simply whimsical reinterpretations of well-known design images. This structure gave me the opportunity to lampoon the format, editorial perspective, and prose style of these publications, as well as have fun playing around with a few dozen graphic icons.

Print magnanimously granted me total freedom in writing, designing, directing, and producing the entire thirteen-page piece. For this, the magazine has my undying respect and admiration, especially considering it was one of my targets.

Reader response was quite gratifying. I received heaps of praise from strangers as well as sycophants. Steve Heller said, "It is without a doubt the funniest thing in the issue." When *Print* received its National Magazine Award, the Managing Editor told me my piece was a major contributing factor. And best of all, the comment made by one of the writers I'd satirically skewered—that I'm "a dead man"—was apparently meant in jest. Whew!

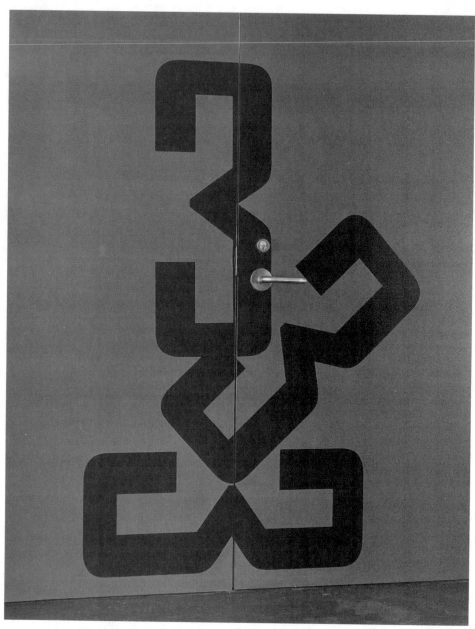

Interior graphics by Paula Scher for The New 42nd Street Studios involve huge displays of type and image placed strategically throughout the building (which make it hard to miss the restrooms).

Paula **Scher**

ON NO ONE GETS LOST

How would you define humor?
Humor is truth turned upside-down, inside-out, magnified, reduced, or backwards.

How would you then define graphic design humor?
Truth turned upside-down, inside-out, magnified, reduced, or backwards.

What makes design funny?
Honesty and surprise.

Is funny the quintessence of graphic humor, or is there some other attribute?
Some graphic design is hilarious. That tends to be more complicated, illustrative, etc.
Some is merely witty or whimsical; those are usually simpler solutions.

What is the most humorous piece of graphic design you have ever seen?

I laugh the most over cartoons. The old *National Lampoon* cartoon of a man in a fancy restaurant sitting next to an enormous fly ordering a long incredibly epicurean repast from an obsequious waiter and ending with the request to "bring some shit for my fly."

I think [the Japanese designer] Fukuda's work is humorous but I don't laugh at it. It is witty. I especially enjoy his guns that that manage to shoot the bullets back into themselves. His work and the fly cartoon work the same way. They take a truth and exaggerate or invert it.

Well, one of the wittiest examples of your work are the signs for the New 42nd Street Studios, a beautiful contemporary building on Times Square that is brilliantly illuminated on the outside and hilariously signed on the inside. Your typography is on the floors, walls, ceilings, and it overtly and by its surprising scale and juxtaposition not only takes the viewers off guard, but makes them think, smile, and indeed laugh. How did this come about?

Architect Charles Platt had designed a rehearsal studio building that felt like a modern-day [twentieth-century Dutch modern] deStjil factory for actors and actresses. The institution's director, Cora Cahan had felt that while the rehearsal studios were modern, spare, and airy, the passageways needed kinetic activity. I noted that actors and actresses learn their stage positions from the floor and that that would be good place to position the directional signage. When the floors proved too small for large-scale messaging, I continued the type on the doors or the walls. The signage is absurd, but it actually functions. No one gets lost and everyone is amused in the process.

Books from Allworth Press

The Graphic Design Reader by Steven Heller (paperback with flaps, 5½ × 8½, 320 pages, $19.95)

The Education of a Design Entrepreneur edited by Steven Heller (paperback, 6¾ × 9⅞, 288 pages, $21.95)

The Education of an E-Designer edited by Steven Heller (paperback, 6¾ × 9⅞, 352 pages, $21.95)

The Education of a Graphic Designer edited by Steven Heller (paperback, 6¾ × 9⅞, 288 pages, $18.95)

Design Issues: How Graphic Design Informs Society edited by DK Holland (paperback, 6¾ × 9⅞, 288 pages, $21.95)

Looking Closer 4: Critical Writings on Graphic Design edited by Michael Bierut, William Drenttel, and Steven Heller (paperback, 6¾ × 9⅞, 304 pages, $21.95)

Graphic Design History edited by Steven Heller and Georgette Balance (6¾ × 9⅞, 352 pages, $21.95)

Graphic Design and Reading: Explorations of an Uneasy Relationship edited by Gunnar Swanson (paperback, 6¾ × 9⅞, 256 pages, $19.95)

The Elements of Graphic Design: Space, Unity, Page Architecture, and Type by Alex W. White (paperback, 6⅛ × 9¼, 160 pages, $24.95)

Starting Your Career As a Freelance Illustrator or Graphic Designer, Revised Edition by Michael Fleishman (paperback, 6 × 9, 272 pages, $19.95)

Inside the Business of Graphic Design: 60 Leaders Share Their Secrets of Success by Catharine Fishel (paperback, 6 × 9, 288 pages, $19.95)

AIGA Professional Practices in Graphic Design: The American Institute of Graphic Arts edited by Tad Crawford (paperback, 6¾ × 9⅞, 320 pages, $24.95)

Business and Legal Forms for Graphic Designers, Revised Edition by Tad Crawford and Eva Doman Bruck (paperback, 8½ × 11, 240 pages, includes CD-ROM, $24.95)

The Graphic Designer's Guide to Pricing, Estimating, and Budgeting, Revised Edition by Theo Stephan Williams (paperback, 6¾ × 9⅞, 208 pages, $19.95)

Careers By Design: A Business Guide for Graphic Designers, Third Edition by Roz Goldfarb (paperback, 6 × 9, 232 pages, $19.95)

Licensing Art and Design, Revised Edition by Caryn R. Leland (paperback, 6 × 9, 128 pages, $16.95)

Please write to request our free catalog. To order by credit card, call 1-800-491-2808 or send a check or money order to Allworth Press, 10 East 23rd Street, Suite 510, New York, NY 10010. Include $5 for shipping and handling for the first book ordered and $1 for each additional book. Ten dollars plus $1 for each additional book if ordering from Canada. New York State residents must add sales tax.

To see our complete catalog on the World Wide Web, or to order online, you can find us at *www.allworth.com*.